# Port Kembla

## A Memoir

Pam Menzies spent the first 16 years of her life in Port Kembla. She now lives in Sydney and has previously published essays in magazines and anthologies, including 'What took me so long?' in *Women of a Certain Age* (Fremantle Press, 2018). This is her first book.

# Port Kembla

## A MEMOIR

PAM MENZIES

ARCADIA

First published 2019 by ARCADIA
*the general books imprint of*
Australian Scholarly Publishing Ltd
7 Lt Lothian St Nth, North Melbourne, Vic 3051
Tel: 03 9329 6963 / Fax: 03 9329 5452
enquiry@scholarly.info / www.scholarly.info

ISBN 978-1-925801-59-0



*Cover artwork:* Zoya Kuptsova and Ryan Phung (2015) 'Billy Cart Derby' [screenprint]. Editioned by Thomas Goulder at Duck Print Fine Art Limited Editions for the 2015 Port Kembla Billy Cart Derby.

*Cover design* Wayne Saunders

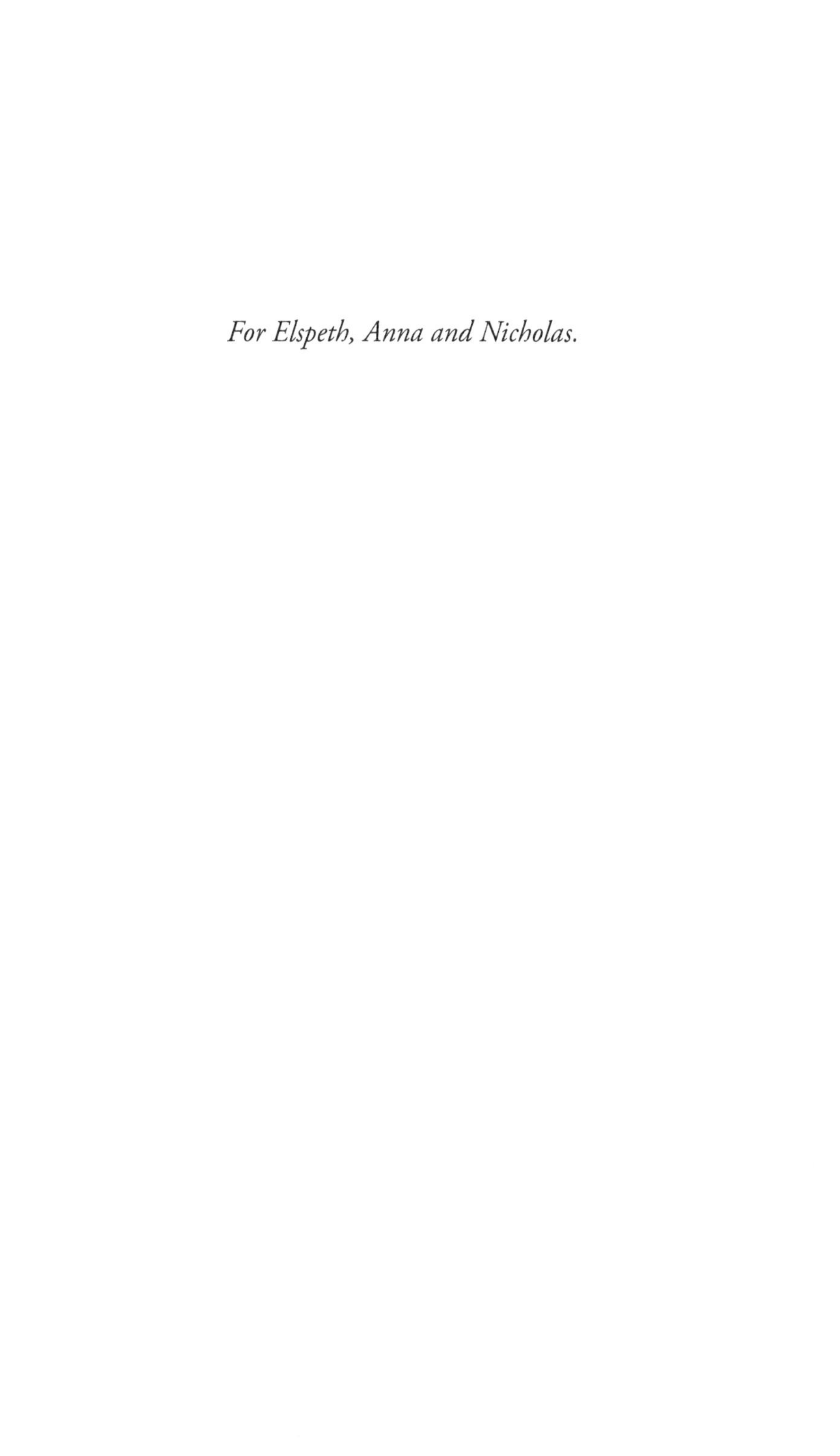

*For Elspeth, Anna and Nicholas.*

# Contents

# Foreword

His Excellency General The Honourable
David Hurley AC DSC, Governor of New South Wales

As a child, Port Kembla was the centre of my universe—its sports teams, social clubs, industry, shopping and general business provided all that I needed.

As I grew I began to understand the importance of Port Kembla as a port and heavy industry location to the local, State and Australian economy. When older, I appreciated my experiences in this multicultural community where I'd eaten spaghetti and drunk red wine well before the rest of Australia became aware of their joy. This book brings back all those memories and more. It retells the experiences of my family and countless other families who worked and lived in Port Kembla and the surrounding townships.

The Port Kembla community is indebted to Pam Menzies for her diligent research, broad reach across community experiences and obvious love for the town, its people and its history. Every chapter sparks a thought, a memory from my own or my parents' and grandparents' experiences.

*Port Kembla: A Memoir* is a valuable addition to the family of local community history books that remind us of our past, of what made us strong as a country and provides thought for our future. The 'Stack' might be gone but the memories the image of it provokes are enduring.

# Maps

During the twentieth century entrepreneurial types sniffed out Port Kembla's industrial potential and with a bevy of excavators, dredges, trenchers and backhoe loaders dug and blasted the town to suit their purposes. Changing Port Kembla's geography changed its history, so maps are an important part of my story.

## 1. Before the excavators

In this map, Illawarra Farm marks the spot of the future Port Kembla. Tom Thumb Lagoon has not yet caught the eye of BHP executives looking for an inner harbour safe from wild south coast weather, Allan's Creek is still winding its way to the sea and there's no bridge over the entrance to the Lagoon.

## 2. After the excavators

After 1956 everything changed. Engineers dismantled the bridge and the small, naturally formed Tom Thumb Lagoon was expanded into a huge inner harbour. The original Port Kembla Harbour, at the entrance of the lagoon, became the Outer Harbour. Building the new road south, King Street, completed the changes that affected Port Kembla profoundly.

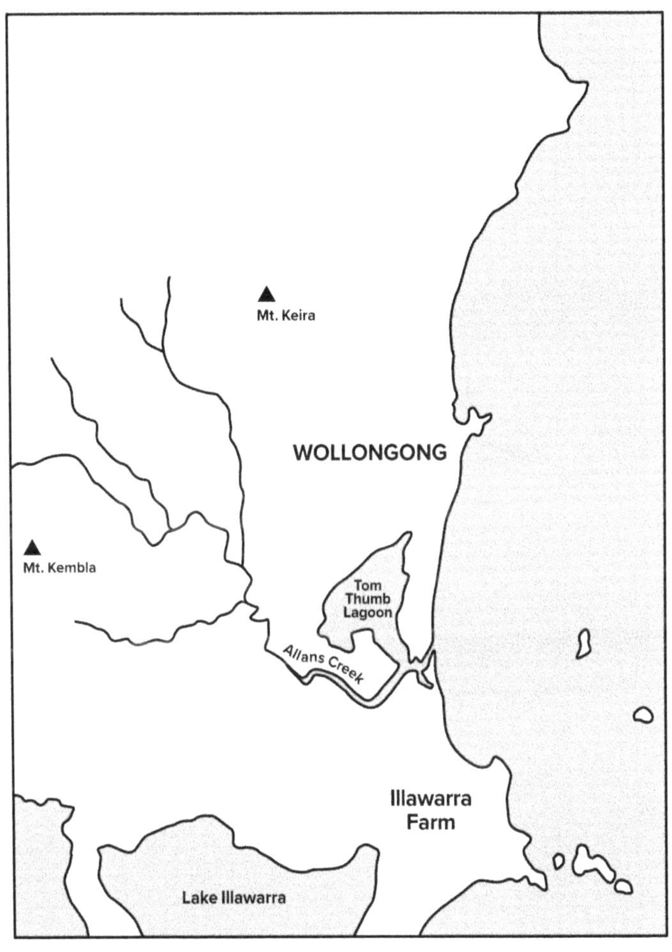
Mt. Keira
WOLLONGONG
Mt. Kembla
Tom
Thumb
Lagoon
Allans Creek
Illawarra
Farm
Lake Illawarra

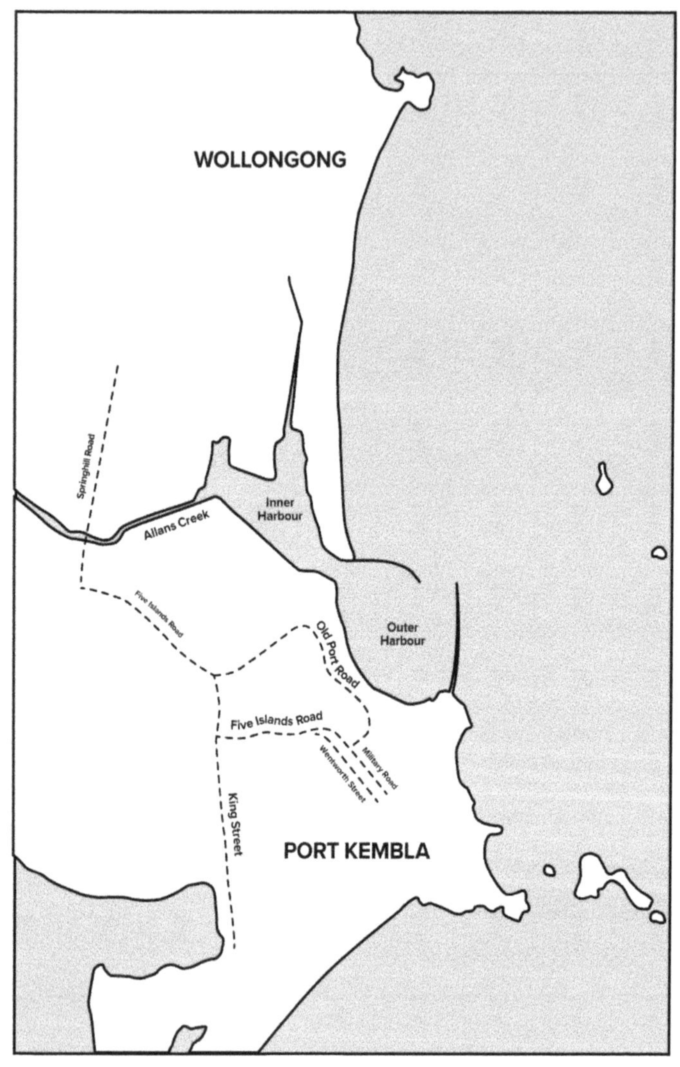

WOLLONGONG
Springhill Road
Inner Harbour
Allans Creek
Five Islands Road
Old Port Road
Outer Harbour
Five Islands Road
Military Road
Wentworth Street
King Street
PORT KEMBLA

# Preface

Readers hoping for a chronological history of Port Kembla will be disappointed with what they find here. I've concentrated on the decades when my family lived in the town. Memory threw up a hotchpotch and I followed its path and the result is an unbalanced account; I have spent more words describing the opening of Port Kembla Public School than either world war because the school was part of my family life while the wars were distant.

In October 2017 my brother David was near death in Port Kembla Hospital. I sat by his bed with his wife and three sons. Looking out the window towards Lake Illawarra, where David had sailed his yachts as a boy, brought back memories. I began describing incidents from his childhood, trying to distract us from our sadness, and realised I was the keeper of the family stories – there was no one else to tell them. That's a powerful role to have. The details of our lives are important, not just to our families but to everyone who wants to know what life was like in a particular place at a particular time. We all need to write stuff down.

PART ONE

# My Port Kembla

# 1
# Remembering

As a teenager I couldn't wait to leave Port Kembla. I read English novels set in atmospheric villages full of witty people surrounded by velvety-green land. My reality was entirely different: fertiliser and smelting businesses, the comings and goings of a busy port, and breathing toxic smoke when the nor'easterly blew. On my way to school in Wollongong, travelling by bus through the clanking, polluted Steelworks, I held my breath, pretending to do my Latin homework. I wanted to be somewhere else, and so did my family. When I was 16, work began on our new house on rain-forested Mount Keira, 16 kilometres to the north. It would take a year to be ready. In the meantime we lived in a friend's house in West Wollongong: two storeys with balconies overlooking a rose-filled garden – just right for a fantasist like me.

Years later, it's Port Kembla that rises to the surface of my mind: not just the place but the characters, many of them eccentric, and a way of life I realise was rich and varied and now long gone. I want to go back and see what's different and look for evidence of things I remember: Port Kembla Public

School, which I hated, and St Stephen's Church, the venue for many family events. I want to find the houses where my friends and I lived and retrace childhood steps. Not far from our house was Private Lane, which you entered from Military Road. This was a magical place, enclosed and inviting. I remember a gate leading in, then first on the right was the Evanses' house, book-filled, with elegant, worn furniture. Further along were timber houses with rambling gardens and on the left, a park and tennis court. I can hear the sound of tennis balls hitting rackets as our mothers played, taste the treats found in my mother's bag in the old wooden shed, and enjoy my speedy self as I run in and out of adjoining houses, playing never-ending games. The smell of warm dusty earth and something else pervades everything.

I looked forward to dinners at the Evanses': they were urbane, relaxed, entertaining. Nothing like this happened at my house. Mr Evans, in jokey mood, would reverse the home movies playing on large spools. We couldn't believe it when everyone walked backwards and jumped out of swimming pools. It's hard to believe that on the other side of the lush trees and shrubs of Private Lane, three industries took up a huge swathe of land bordered by the ocean: ER&S, Metal Manufactures and Australian Fertilisers. They were the noisy, smelly workplaces of our fathers. The Lane was on company land and the houses were for employees. Somehow I've kept the memory of the oasis and blanked out the rest.

My earliest memories of life are in Robertson Street, on top of a Port Kembla hill. By swivelling my head I could see harbour, beach or lake. With selective vision, shutting out Australian Fertilisers, Metal Manufactures, ER&S and the huge meccano-set structures of the Steelworks, it was spectacular. There was no Warrawong or Berkeley to the west; just green land. Sky and water, ever-changing colour according to their moods, tempered the man-made ugliness. That's where it began, my love of living on hills.

Recently in the *Sydney Morning Herald* I read about Port Kembla being hit by a turbulent storm, and I remember the weather as a dominant force in my childhood. The town's geography attracted winds from every direction. Some we liked and others we didn't. When dust and hot air came on the wings of a westerly, we retreated inside and closed the windows. The southerly buster brought thunder, lightning and often torrential rain and was mostly welcomed because it brought relief from summer heat. The favourite wind of all was the nor'easterly, a light afternoon breeze that gave us cool nights for sleeping.

Through wind and rain and fumy air we walked. We didn't have much choice. It wasn't until I was ten that my father bought a black Morris Oxford car. It was two kilometres to school and church, about one to the main street for shopping and over two to the beach. When you live on a hill it's a long slog home. My sensory memory is full of trudges from the shops with my mother. Wentworth Street, the main street, was a prosperous place in the 1950s with assorted businesses up and down the roller-coaster hill. There was Mr Kemp the grocer, always dressed in a suit and tie, his goods displayed in hessian sacks: rice and flour, sugar and tea, their aromas part of the atmosphere of the shop. He weighed everything on elaborate scales and packed them into paper bags. He also came to our house each week to take delivery orders. Fairleys, the haberdasher, had a grander place, built in my grandmother's day. Everything you could think of was separated into aisles for easy viewing. In early photos of the town it's easily seen at the top of the street and the building remains today, although in a reduced state. We'd pass the Whiteway, modelled on a glamorous Manly cinema, which was the centre of entertainment life before television. However, what I waited for was the cake shop and the Napoleon slices: layers of soft sponge cake, jam, cream and crunchy passionfruit pastry. And what I really wanted was a little chick, on sale every Friday at the greengrocers, but my mother always ignored my pleas. I would say, 'Just one, it won't take up much space.' Time and again I got nowhere. My mother was inured to my pleas: years of chooks and a mouse phobia left her unimpressed – in her mind hens equalled mice.

Every afternoon after school from the age of about six there was another walk I disliked. The first part was fine: I was happy to be out of the two-storey, liver-brick block of Port Kembla Public School adjacent to the industrial chimneys spewing smoke. There was a group of four or five of us, dressed in our tunics and carrying globite cases. Sometimes we called in to the library at the top of Wentworth Street and tussled over the latest book, at other times we went straight to the corner shop for our favourite fix: lemon sherbets with licorice straws in triangular packets. Often we didn't have to pay because the shop belonged to our friend Lyn's father. In summer we stocked up on lemonade or raspberry ice blocks at a shop further along our route at the bottom of Keira Street. After trudging up the hill we would reach Bland Street where my cousin Diana lived; she was home – lucky her. Not me, and Billy Harris's gang was waiting – a bunch of boys my age who morphed into afternoon warriors. They hid behind large clumps of dry grass on a vacant block and were hard to spot in their summer camouflage of brown faces and bleached hair. Most afternoons I sprinted round the corner into Robertson Street accompanied by shouts and flying stones. What was my mother thinking, dressing me in viyella blouses with Peter Pan collars, plaiting my hair and tying it with ribbons in an industrial town on the south coast in the 1950s? Of course I was a target! However, it prepared me for later on. In Sixth Class at my new school in Wollongong I won the catch-the-train race at the annual sports day. It was my favourite event: we ran to the end of the athletics field in sports clothes, put on our whole uniform, including stockings, gloves and hat, and raced back to the start.

My cousin Diana and I returned to Port Kembla in 1999 for the 50-year reunion of our kindergarten class. We were nervous about our reception. Did we dare tell them that the hated ER&S stack, still standing at this stage, had been built on Uncle Harry's watch? Had they forgiven us for leaving in Fifth Class to attend another school in Wollongong? Would Billy Harris be there? Would the whole visit be a disaster? We entered the cramped but friendly space, pinned on name tags bearing our original surnames and checked our kindergarten class for signs of weathering. A tall man approached and I looked at his name tag – William Harris. Surely not. This tall, well-dressed person could not be Billy. He gave me his card which confirmed he was indeed Billy Harris and now owned a trucking business.

'Why did you throw stones at me?'

'Because I liked you.'

2

# 2015: Going back

No stack, no school, no house, no Whiteway Picture Theatre, no Fairleys, no nothing; most of what I remember has been obliterated. I'm back with my husband, John, in Port Kembla after many years and the day is hot and humid. The town sits on a collection of small hills and we drive down and up the steep main street, parking near St Stephen's at the top. The church is smaller than I remember, with its pitched roof and liver-brick walls. It's very much locked and I ring the number on the notice board and find out it's a part-time church with a part-time pastor. They would come from Dapto, 15 kilometres away, to open it but are short staffed today. Maybe another time? The property looks sad, there's a car park that used to be a garden where we played after Sunday school; the old rectory looks like a rental – mattresses piled up in the glassed-in verandah. The place hasn't been painted in a while and the garden is overgrown. At least the preschool on the other side of the church is full of life. The church hall still looks impressive, which fits my memory of its importance in my life.

Looking down Military Road to the north, the Steelworks is a still-life on the horizon until smoke begins puffing from a chimney, suggesting the coke ovens are quenching. I cross the road from St Stephen's to where Port Kembla Public School used to be and find nothing but concrete slabs, old rusted wire fences and long grass. Now there are only birds making any noise and all we can see are abandoned industrial buildings. ER&S, Metal Manufactures, Australian Fertilisers – all gone. However, the ocean has reasserted its beauty and I breathe in air much sweeter than I remember. My emotions are jangling, vivid memories jump out of my brain, yet there's nothing here.

We walk towards a building at the top of Wentworth Street which used to be the library and essential to my childhood. Now it's the Port Kembla Community Centre and I'm keen to buy a copy of *Tender*, the film made about their cut-price funeral project which I'd seen at the Sydney Film Festival.[1] Everyone is away today except Tina. She tells me about the film's success, which includes awards at film festivals in New York and London. There's a lot of support in the area for cut-price funerals but no money, according to Tina.

The film is one of the main reasons I'm back in town. I was bowled over by both the film and its supporters at the Festival. The excitement in the cinema that day was palpable. Everyone was calling out to each other and a man with a dog was sitting in the front row. Wanting to be part of it I told the woman behind me that I was born in Port Kembla. She gave me a pat.

The film began and I was hooked. A group of women are discussing plans to deliver cut-price funerals. The response to one man who dares question them sets the tone: 'We're not going to wheel in bucket loads of sawdust to fix the orifices. It's not taxidermy!' They're gutsy, humorous, open and critical of multinational funeral businesses that they say are ripping everyone off. They want to reclaim the process. The place where it's all happening is the Port Kembla Community Centre run by Jenny Briscoe-Hough. In the film we meet Misty, Ann, and Lorraine from the Coomaditchie Aboriginal group, Andrew with his dog Bailey, and Nigel, who has made it his job to look after them all. The can't-be-ignored presence is industry, whose smoke hangs over the town. The soundtrack booms, reinforcing a sense of menace as grey clouds roll overhead. Andrew says, 'I couldn't wait to get out. It's alive, rumbling like a big monster.' Lynette Wallworth, the director, keeps the focus on the people of the Port and allows them to tell their story honestly, forthrightly. I walk out of the cinema wanting to reconnect with this place.

Now I'm back, all I can think about is lunch. We head for the Red Kitchen at Tina's suggestion. John says walking down Wentworth Street is like walking onto a film set: no one is around and most of the buildings are boarded up except for several wedding shops. I try not to look for places I remember because they are simply not there. Lunch is good, as organic as possible, they advertise. We drink strawberry milkshakes without straws because they haven't sourced biodegradable ones yet. We see small shoots of Port Kembla revival in the art shops nearby. However, the busiest place is the barber – people are in and out the whole time we are having lunch. The woman running the cafe says that all they need is more foot traffic. Good luck to them, but later on a quick drive through Warrawong it's clear where all the life's gone. Multiple supermarkets, the usual chains and cinemas have all set up shop there.

I steel myself for a 'high noon' walk down the lifeless street, trying to be grown up about time moving on and change being inevitable, etc. This doesn't stop my gasp when I see the clear, grass-covered space where the Whiteway Picture Theatre used to be. I have spent months re-imagining my childhood and getting ready to write about it. Now I wonder if I am up to being confronted by the present-day reality. I find out later that the Whiteway burnt down in 1992. Port Kembla Public School was also lost to fire, torched in the early hours of 4 January 2013. A witness described it as a massive inferno.[2]

I'm relieved the banks and pubs are still here anchoring the corners, though the pubs have different names and the banks different purposes. I take too many photos, relieved when I find something I remember. Otherwise my eye goes to the facades above the awnings, looking for remnants. I don't find much, but am happy to see 'entra Chambers 1937' has only two letters missing. Today, the Local Court in Darcy Road, at the Steelworks end of town, is busy. The manager of a Wollongong hotel has been charged with a drink-driving offence while driving his boss's sports car.

We leave Wentworth Street, drive past the old National Bank and up the hill towards where I lived as a child. The corner shop has gone, the place where I'd buy an ice block to help me get to the top. Not only has my childhood house disappeared but the house numbers have changed. I begin to doubt myself and when I return home check the number on the small wooden school case I still have and yes, it is definitely 13. It's odd, we owned two blocks of land and now there are two houses built on these, both numbered 12. I look for evidence of the houses of families I remember. The Mortons' house opposite is still there, but it has 13 marked on its gate, and the houses of the Millses, Darlings, Harpers and Thompsons remain. The street still has its wonderful vantage point with panoramic views of sea and lake. By the looks of things it is much sought after. The newer houses are different from the 1950s versions, lovingly decorated with columns, balconies and pot plants.

No-longer-vacant blocks, additions, dilapidations and other changes confuse and question my memory. It's tiring dealing with disappointment and loss. I'm momentarily cheered by the sight of a circus tent down by the lake – a blast from my past – before heading for one last sweep through the streets. In my mind I've packed up the town as a forgotten, gone-to-seed place. However, that's before I visit the pool and the new primary school. Seven million dollars have been spent on the pool complex. I'm surprised at this evidence of government commitment. Three renovated pools, free entry and uncrowded, it's the place to be. I look out over the rock platform and the beach – a long, lazy arch of sand stretching towards blue-grey hills – and feel a rush of unexpected pride. This is reinforced when I drive past the well-designed low-rise school with its view of islands and sea.

Before I leave, there is one more place I want to find: Private Lane. I know it's long gone, but hope for something. As we drive down Military Road, parallel to Wentworth Street and towards the Steelworks, I catch sight of a wooden gate on the right that pricks my memory. When we stop I see an overgrown tennis court. It's like much of Port Kembla, another dilapidated site with abandoned work buildings and old wire fencing. However, I'm relieved, sensing this is it, and pat the gate in acknowledgement, grateful for something. There are no houses left, nothing except the gate and the court, but it's the site, I'm sure. Hard to believe this is where Lew Hoad and Ken Rosewall, at one time the world's greatest players, gave a demonstration tennis match in Port Kembla's halcyon 1950s.

I want to find the old road to Wollongong which was our link to the outside world. I grew up listening to my mother Audrey's stories about Darcy, the temperamental horse, and the public coach to Wollongong which was drawn by several horses. Audrey remembered riding in the coach in semi-darkness because there were no windows, just rolled-up oilcloth blinds which were usually drawn because of the weather. In 1920, at the age of six, she went by herself on the coach to see third cousins in Wollongong and was put in the charge of the driver; she couldn't take her eyes off the hook that replaced his hand. She wondered how he'd lost it – down the coal mine, on the wharf or any number of other dangerous South Coast workplaces.

We have little luck tracing the road on the Port Kembla side. It peters out at the Port Authority security gates. No road remains connecting Port Kembla to Wollongong beside the sea because it was severed during the building of the inner harbour. Yet I can't help looking for traces. From the Wollongong end we manage to get closer and see huge piles of coal waiting to be loaded onto ships. Security is tight.

South Coast visionaries had their eye on this huge lagoon of protected water from the early days. William Wiley, Wollongong's mayor, was the first to make a development proposition in 1887. The Public Works department drew up their plan in 1916. However, it wasn't until 1955, with the passing of the *Inner Harbour Act*, that dredging began. Six days a week, using three dredges, they scooped out and disposed of tons of mud. The seventh day was set aside for maintenance. Five years later it opened. The SS *Yampi*, carrying iron ore from Yampi Sound in Western Australia, was the first ship to enter the completed harbour on 28 November 1960.[3]

Stopped by another security gate at the northern side, we stand and watch as tugs chivvy a huge ship carrying cars into position, ready to unload its cargo. Standing there, smelling the coal, hearing the whining, banging industry, gazing at the ageing metal structures, I begin to understand a little of what had given my grandparents and my parents their livelihood. There's an energetic, if repelling, spent force about it. But not so fast – as we leave we count 18 trucks laden with coal waiting to enter the terminal.

3

# 1910: My family comes to town

It was copper, not coal, that kick-started Port Kembla's industrial life, and it was copper that drew my grandfather, Alfred Hartley, who arrived in this still beautiful coastal town 93 kilometres south of Sydney in 1910. He secured a job as an accountant at ER&S – the Electrolytic Refining and Smelting Company. It was a private venture financed by the Mount Morgan Gold Mining Company and a German metallurgical group. They planned to smelt copper and other metals using a new process of electrolysis. With permission from the New South Wales government to build a low jetty, work began in 1908: clearing land, constructing buildings and building railways. The fortunes of the company rose and fell depending on the copper price. For years ER&S provided employment (500 men in 1908) and spawned other industries: Metal Manufactures arrived in 1917 and processed copper into wires, cables and copper pipes, and in 1921 Australian Fertilisers was established and turned the sulphuric acid formed during the copper smelting process into fertiliser.

ER&S is where my grandfather spent all his working life. My uncle Harry also worked there, starting as a junior clerk in 1927 and becoming general manager in 1961. It was during his time in charge, in 1965, that the controversial local landmark the ER&S stack was built, an attempt to push polluting gases higher into the atmosphere and away from local residents. My mother, her sister and her brother Leigh also spent some of their working lives at ER&S. My grandfather and uncle gave 70 years of service between them. Like my father, they only ever worked for a single company. It's hard to understand now, this life-long commitment to one firm and its town, and especially difficult considering the polluting effects of the venture. It was the sulphuric acid in the air that drove my family away in the late 1950s and caused growing resentment among the townsfolk. Although the community was warned in 1908 about sulphur fumes, it welcomed the enterprise – Mr O'Donnell, a local farmer, was one of only a few to publicly object.

Back in 1910 Port Kembla was hurrying to invent itself: the port was busy with steamers loading coal and a coke works was in the process of being built by the Mount Lyell Company. Shops dotted the fledgling main street and the Lifesaving Club and ambulance station were in operation. With dirt tracks and horse and sulky travel, journeys were challenging. Houses were lit with kerosene lamps, and cooking was done on wood-fired stoves. Outside there were laundries with coppers for boiling clothes and toilets with huge pans. It was a dusty, smelly life. The Kembla Amusement and Investment Company provided electricity, though people complained about the cost. The

*Illawarra Mercury* reported that the company was asking £2 10 shillings ($4) per pole.[1] One resident was quoted saying, 'It is ridiculous to make such a request of working men.' There was no street lighting in Wollongong until 1921; not until 1938 were the citizens of Port Kembla invited to a ceremony where street lighting was switched on for the first time at the corner of Wentworth and Allan Streets.

***

My grandmother died three years before I was born. However, I have little trouble conjuring her up thanks to my mother's stories. She was a baker of cakes, flamboyant in her dress, a wearer of hats, a gadabout. I have a picture of her standing in a flowing white dress with my two-year-old mother, also in white. The formality of it intrigues me, living as they did in a town with dirt roads and basic facilities. What was the reason for dressing up? I check the records; the new school was opened in 1917 and there was also a surf carnival in 1917. Did these events warrant long white dresses and large-brimmed hats? What brought my grandmother to Port Kembla? As my mother often told the story of my grandmother Gertrude's elopement to marry Alfred, that's where I'll begin.

Gertrude somehow found the courage to resist family pressure and marry Alfred. Why was Alfred considered not good enough? All I have are my mother's stories of Gertrude's supposed higher social standing (portraits of her forebears hung in Victorian art galleries), but no hard facts. I have a fragment of the faded wedding certificate. In perfect copperplate writing it tells me that Henry Bryant, a Christian minister, performed the marriage of Gertrude May Hughson (21 and a spinster) and Alfred Henry Hartley (26 and trained as an accountant) at 430 Bourke Street, Melbourne, which is now a menswear shop. Also on the certificate are the names of Gertrude's parents, Charles Hughson and Mary McLoughlan, along with the bride's address, Scotchmere Street, North Fitzroy, and her birthplace, Yan Yean, just north of Melbourne.

They were married on 6 June 1894. Did any of Gertrude's family come? There must have been a celebration! Party-loving Gertrude wasn't likely to have sneaked away into the night. Charles, her father, was long dead. Gertrude, the fifth child, was born in the last year of his life in 1873 when he was 41. Charles and two of his brothers came to Australia in the mid-nineteenth century from the Shetland Islands, where their father worked as a sea captain. Charles was listed on the wedding certificate as a road contractor. Somehow 20 years after his death there was still money. My mother remembers cheques arriving for years from Victoria allowing Gertrude to indulge her love of shopping until an accountant embezzled what was left.

With her father dead and in spite of family disapproval Gertrude married Alfred, a young man from Williamstown Victoria. They both loved music, so might have met at a Melbourne concert. (Alfred was in the city to study accountancy.) I know music was important to them as the only paper evidence from their early married lives in Mount

Perry, Queensland, where they moved for Alfred's work, was a receipt for a piano from Beale and Company. The young couple bought an upright piano for 75 guineas on a three-year term with an offer of a ten-guinea discount if they paid it off in three months.

What's amazing for the time is that the piano was completely built in Australia, and the building where it was made still stands at 47 Trafalgar Street, Annandale, in Sydney's inner west. Octavius Charles Beale was the one with the vision. When he visited in 1893, the French music critic Oscar Comettant said, 'No other factory produced nearly as many parts used in piano-making in the British Empire.' And the company was efficient: 95,000 pianos were built between 1893 and 1975.[2]

When Alfred and Gertrude moved to Port Kembla for Alfred's job at ER&S, the Beale piano went with them. It seems unbelievable, in horse and cart days, that the bulky piano travelled from Mount Perry to Port Kembla. Did it come by ship? When the couple arrived in town in 1910 they also brought with them their three children: 14-year-old Charles William Leigh, known in the family as Leigh; Hazel, aged nine; and the baby, Harry Hughson, born in 1909. One more child, my mother Audrey May, was born in Port Kembla in 1914.

They were the lucky ones: with a job, a company house in D'Arcy Road and later enough money to buy a house at 15 Reservoir Street with views of sea and sand. The neat row of D'Arcy Road's wooden houses, all the same design, were built beside the new industries. Today this road lies marooned in an abandoned industrial wasteland on the way to the old harbour. The houses are gone and weeds and industrial detritus are all that remain.

In 1910 life settled into a pattern for the Hartleys with Alfred at work and Gertrude busy at home and increasingly involved with community activities associated with church and the Red Cross. The older children went to school, not that getting there was easy. The old single-room school, which had become full-time in 1901, was dismantled and re-erected on its third site in 1907, and the children needed to cross dangerous railway lines and a lagoon at the mouth of Salty Creek to reach it. A reporter from the *Illawarra Mercury* described the challenges:

> Owing to the height of the water at Salty Creek on Monday, the younger children attending school had to be carried on the backs of the older boys. Some years ago a little girl was drowned in the locality ... The Port Kembla Progress Association, through their secretary, forwarded a telegram to the Minister of Education to the following effect: 'Salty Creek impassable: school on one side and township on the other. Again strongly urge removal of school to centre of township.'[3]

My mother was lucky, by the time she went to school in 1919 the government had heeded the town's call and built a substantial two-storey brick edifice on the hill at the top of Military Road. No longer did the flooded Salty Creek need to be crossed.

Growing up I tuned into my mother's chatter. Even though her parents were long gone I soaked up her childhood by osmosis, the funny stories, the characters, and what mattered to her. Confidence, style and commitment to community were attributes my mother and grandmother shared. I have absorbed much of their love of life. Even Gertrude's table rules made it down the line. I'm uneasy if salt and pepper shakers are still on the table during dessert, or if linen napkins are not provided. Was it the well-ordered home that encouraged Gertrude's family to eventually accept Alfred? Whatever it was, a constant stream of aunts began visiting from Melbourne. At my instigation, Audrey wrote down some of her memories when she was 75:

> Harry and I were most impressed by Great-aunt Sarah, my maternal grandmother's sister. She wore high-necked, black rustling gowns (floor length), commandeered our only rocking chair and made authoritative pronouncements. Our behaviour, for the duration of her visit, was impeccable.

I wonder about the stories we tell about our past and why my mother often talked of her parents' elopement. Perhaps it was the romance of it, or Gertrude's pluckiness in marrying Alfred against family advice. The adventure of travelling to live in Mount Perry, a small Queensland copper town in the 1890s, a long way from family and the bright lights of Melbourne, and then moving to Port Kembla, yet still managing to forge a successful life, was also likely to have captured my mother's imagination.

Darcy was another one of Audrey's favourite stories. Back in my grandparents' time, if you wanted to travel there was often a temperamental horse to deal with, and first you had to catch him. Darcy opened gates with his teeth and ate neighbours' vegetables. He was allowed to find grazing within a reasonable distance from home, as they couldn't stop him even if they'd wanted to. When the family needed transport, they'd ask people in the town if anyone had seen him. Pretending he was out for a stroll, my grandfather would approach Darcy holding a rope behind his back and apples and bread in front of him. Darcy, wised up to this ploy, would show little interest. After several attempts he would be caught and attached to the sulky ready for the trip to Wollongong, the main destination about 15 kilometres away. The lure for my grandmother was Lances, the department store. (David Jones took it over in 1960.) The original road from Port Kembla passed by the harbour, full of ships loading coal from the Mount Kembla mine, and then crossed Tom Thumb Lagoon via a wooden bridge where water lapped close during high tides. Darcy was mostly happy on the road. However, if a steam roller appeared he reared and sometimes bolted.

After my grandmother had bought her hats, veils and haberdashery items, Mr Lance (born 1840), dressed in frock coat and gloves, would be ready to hand her and my mother into the sulky. However, Darcy would have other ideas – once he was harnessed, he had no intention of stopping. My grandfather raced the sulky up and down Crown and Burelli Streets, hoping to stop long enough for his wife and daughter to jump in, which they did, usually with legs grazed. Eventually Darcy was replaced by Jack, who halted when necessary but also hated steam rollers. I'm sure Walter Lance empathised with my grandfather. I found out via Walter's obituary, which appeared in the *Illawarra Mercury* on 18 October 1929, that in his home town of Birmingham, England, he had been a keen hunter. After a riding accident he was advised to come to Australia for health reasons. The sight of out-of-control Darcy on Burelli Street no doubt stirred up old memories.

***

Nothing much remains of my grandparents' lives. I have a few photographs, and love the early ones of my grandmother's picnics. There are women in filmy blouses and long skirts, men in three-piece suits and bowler hats. They sit on picnic rugs in the middle of the bush. Audrey, at three or four, looks cute in a flouncy white dress with her hair in corkscrew curls, while brother Harry is dressed like the men. They are at their favourite picnic spot at Mount Keira, where their friends the Ansteys were school teachers. Mount Kembla and Mount Keira are familiar landmarks, rising out of the green escarpment behind Wollongong like two hats, one rounded, the other flat. To get to the picnic my family had to first catch the horse and attach it to the sulky. My mother always said she much preferred sulky travel to cars. Imagining their clip-clopping journey, enjoying the landscape before high UV levels, I can see the appeal.

One time my grandparents travelled with a neighbouring couple in two sulkies up Macquarie Pass, across to Cambewarra Pass, down to Nowra and home. The attraction was the contrast of cool, temperate rainforests full of towering eucalypts and ferns after the heat of the coastal plain. At the slow pace of sulky travel they may have seen lyrebirds darting across roads or potoroos and tiger quolls foraging in the thick mulch under the tree canopy. Both passes were (and remain) a challenge for drivers, winding sharply through thick rainforest, and the waterfalls made conditions slippery, especially after rain. For my grandparents the journey took two weeks, with nights spent at guesthouses. My mother remembers being relieved when they returned. Now the whole journey can be done by car before lunch.

As I attempt to piece together life in early Port Kembla and search for evidence of my grandparents, I am frustrated by the lack of anything that proves or disproves my mother's stories. Everyone who knew them is long dead and they wrote nothing down. Finally I find something, Gertrude's obituary in the *South Coast Times and Wollongong Argus* dated Friday, 19 April 1940. On page 15, in an article headed 'Port Kembla', there is news of a cycle club outing, last Saturday's marriage of Bertha Lee to John Thompson (friends of my parents) and a social afternoon organised by the Returned Soldiers Ladies

Auxiliary. In the last sentence, Gertrude is mentioned:

> After a long illness Mrs Gertrude May Hartley, wife of Mr Alfred Hartley, died on Monday. She was 65 years of age and had been a resident of Port Kembla for 30 years. She had interested herself in many local organisations particularly C of E work, Red Cross and Boy Scout activities. She is survived by a husband and family of 4.

This gives me a sense of her: a lively, involved woman. Just four months later, on Friday, 16 August 1940, the *Illawarra Mercury* reported:

> Port Kembla lost one of its oldest and best known residents last Saturday when the death occurred of Mr Alfred Henry Hartley at the age of 73. The deceased came from Mount Perry Queensland and for over 30 years was engaged at the ER&S works as departmental manager.

My grandparents made it into print – a pity it had to wait until their obituaries, but I now have concrete evidence they lived in Port Kembla as it developed into an industrial powerhouse.

## 4

# Other people in the landscape

The site of the future town caught the eye of Captain James Cook as he swung round a rocky outcrop in 1770. He liked what he saw and named it 'Red Point'. His job was to report back to London on every new variety of man, plant and beast. Seeing figures on shore he wanted to get closer. When the yawl, a two-masted fore-and-aft rigged sailing boat, was finally launched (probably somewhere near Woonona, just north of Wollongong) with Joseph Banks and Daniel Solander aboard, they struggled but still couldn't land 'by reason of the great surf that beat everywhere upon the shore.'[1] All Cook could do was observe the local inhabitants from afar, and note that their small canoes looked much like the ones he'd seen in New Zealand, before filling his sails and heading north. We now know that those sighted were the Wadi-Wadi people of Dharwal country.

By 1796 George Bass and Matthew Flinders were in the area, also floundering about and trying to land in their boat, the *Tom Thumb*. By now there had been enough interaction between the different peoples to cause mutual distrust. Flinders wrote of his fear of cannibals. However, with no fresh water, spoiled provisions and Bass badly sunburnt, they accepted the offer of water and two fish from men who said they were from Port Jackson. The men guided them to what historians now believe was a spot south of the town, probably Lake Illawarra and not the inner harbour which has since become known as Tom Thumb Lagoon. Bass and Flinders dried their muskets, loaded the boat up with water and mended a broken oar. They also had time for closer interaction with the local people. Flinders describes a hair-cutting session in his diary. After the two Aboriginal guides had shown off the haircuts Flinders had given them, the other men wanted the same.

> Some of the more timid were alarmed at a double-jawed instrument coming so close to their noses, and could scarcely be persuaded by their shaven friends to allow the operation to be finished but when their chins were held up a second time, their fear of the instrument, the wild stare of their eyes – the smile which they forced – formed a compound upon the rough, savage countenance not unworthy of a Hogarth.[2]

However, becoming increasingly suspicious of their guides, who were encouraging them to bring the boat further into the lake, Bass and Flinders lost their cool, fired their freshly dry muskets and quickly left for Port Jackson.

Even though South Coast Aboriginal people did everything to help early explorers and settlers, showing them tracks down mountains where the good grazing land was for cattle and introducing them to their women, their needs were ignored. Their land was parcelled out to pastoralists like goods for sale, revealed in this letter written in 1816 by Colonial Secretary John Campbell to the Surveyor-General, John Oxley:

> The Governor has no objection to Mr Allan receiving an exact equivalent in Illawarra for those lands he now possesses in Upper Minto or Airds.[3]

In January 1822 Governor Macquarie met with 100 Aboriginal people on Mr Allan's land. They came to welcome him to the Illawarra. The governor described them as 'civil' and regretted that he hadn't brought some tobacco to distribute. Unbeknown to these first inhabitants, life as they knew it was over. First seen by Captain Cook and now appropriated by Governor Macquarie, the Illawarra was opening up for white man's business. Over the next hundred years in the name of progress all the land of this 'civil' people was systematically 'redistributed' and they were reduced to living on the edge of white people's lives.

When pale-skinned residents arrived in the nineteenth century, Indigenous people were on the beaches and in the hills surrounding Port Kembla, gathering food, telling stories and carrying out their ceremonies. Middens and burial sites in the area are evidence that they had done this for thousands of years. They called the place Illowra, land of beauty and plenty. The sea was full of mullet, black fish, bream and leather jacket, and in the rock pools there were pipis and abalone. They were expert fishermen and had a thriving industry set up on the Port Kembla point, complete with holding pools for caught fish.

Early in the twentieth century, Illowra, or Hill 60 as it became known, was still a perfect ecosystem. The coming of white people upset the balance between the original inhabitants and their environment. Trees and bushes, often sources of food, were cut down, roads and houses built over hunting grounds, and fishing habits challenged. Compounding the breakdown in their daily rituals, the men were lured into the world of paid white work on the wharves, in hotels and driving trucks, and were introduced to alcohol.

In the 1920s my mother, Audrey, was aware of the camps on Hill 60 and around the town and the Aboriginal children at the local school, but she wasn't allowed to have anything to do with them. Parents didn't approve of the pustules they saw on Aboriginal legs and kept their children away. But Audrey often watched the fishermen at Fishermans Beach:

> The Aboriginal community living on Hill 60 provided the district with fresh fish. Each day a lookout was posted on top of the hill overlooking the beach to signal to the tribe when a shoal was sighted. The boats were launched and hauls of flapping fish were expertly netted. The fish came around the point through a narrow channel. Word of a haul spread quickly to the townspeople and the catch sold promptly.

Queen Rosie did my grandparents' washing and Audrey remembers her smiling face and gentle ways. She also remembers Queen Rosie's husband, King Billy, dressed in a serge suit and walking carefully up Wentworth Street after a drinking session. Except for the mutually satisfactory trade in fish, misunderstanding, neglect and injustice appear to sum up Port Kembla's response to its first inhabitants. Exemplifying this in 1923 was the annexing of the lower part of Hill 60, where Indigenous people had lived for so long, for a golf course.

One of my clearest childhood memories is of being on a cliff above the beach with friends and watching the descendants of the fishermen Audrey had known picking fish out of their nets. Our parents would be playing golf nearby and we'd be ranging about. Fishermans Beach was always our first stop because that's where our favourite sandhills were – steep rollercoasters of warm sand. I remember the thrill of the fast spin towards water. By the time I was a child, the Aboriginal camp had been moved away. In 1941 the Department of Defence took over Hill 60, renaming it Kembla Fortress. The military advantage of its clear sightlines up and down the coast and out to sea was too good to be ignored.

In spite of the general disregard for Indigenous peoples, there are echoes of them in the names of the South Coast towns: Bulli, Kembla, Wollongong, Warrawong, Unanderra, Kiama and Nowra.

Muriel Davis, an Indigenous woman who lived in Port Kembla at the same time I did, says it wasn't all bad. 'We used to go to the Whiteway Picture Theatre ... We could sit anywhere we chose, not like from Nowra to Bega where Kooris weren't allowed in pubs and had to sit up the front at picture theatres. Things were different in the Illawarra because of the protection from wharfies and the coal miners who would strike through their unions to look after fellow workers. Kooris in the camps were respected by the white people. We were always dressed nice when we went into town shopping. Wentworth Street was the busiest little street then.'

And yet, as in most places in Australia at that time, she also remembers bruising treatment by whites. 'My father talked about a police sergeant who was transferred from Goodooga to Port Kembla. When he saw a lot of Kooris in the hotels he kicked them out and warned the publicans never to serve them. But the quick retaliation by the combined unions saw the racial decision overturned and that particular policeman transferred away from Port Kembla.'[4]

5

# Boom times round the corner

Layers of concrete and time disguise evidence of how the town was brought to life. My bower-bird mind wants to make sense of the remnants. Estragon and Vladimir in *Waiting for Godot* talk about dead voices making a noise like wings.[1] I'm hearing the wings and trying to cobble the sound into a story. But I'll need to listen carefully if I'm to unearth the town's, and my family's, lives. Rummaging through old photos, looking for a conduit, I find an early panoramic shot of the town and note the harbour, the new breakwater and a largish hall. There are houses dotted about but only a few trees. Who cut them down – was it the timber-getters? The cedar trees were prized for furniture-making. The houses look similar, each with a pitched roof, a front verandah and two windows either side of the front door. Wooden fences stake their claim around the houses and two chimney stacks are sending up smoke. A tiny church is part of the mix, as is the impressive bulk of Fairleys haberdashery at the northern end of the main street. And the school is there, at the very right-hand edge of the photo, so it must have been taken after 1916. Unlike European towns, the buildings are positioned randomly: there's no clustering around a church or a square or a sandy cove with atmospheric boats bobbing.

The outdoor dunnies are plonked down at a distance from the houses, keeping flies and strong smells at a distance. As a child, the worst thing that could happen was the dunny man arriving while I was inside the corrugated-iron structure, perched over the pan's maggoty contents. They did their best, whistling loudly, dressed in their shorts and navy-blue singlets, a fresh pail on their shoulders. They ran along special lanes beside the houses that were designed for the purpose. My cousin Diana never forgot the day a truck carrying full pails tipped sideways in Bland Street near her house, spilling the putrid contents.

***

The harbour was an early focus during the town's boom phase. Since 1883 there had been a jetty, known as the Kembla Jetty, which had been built to ship coal from the Mount Kembla mine, about 20 kilometres away. But it wasn't enough – locals wanted more and were prepared to fight for it. In 1896, the *Illawarra Mercury* reported that a 'monster deputation' met with the Minister of Public Works, Mr Young, demanding a deepwater port for the Illawarra. Mayors, heads of businesses and interested parties turned up in droves and wouldn't take no for an answer. Mr Beetson, Mayor of Wollongong, said the Illawarra possessed mountains of coal and many other natural resources which couldn't be developed because there wasn't a suitable harbour. John Payne, Mayor of North Illawarra, and others wondered about certain parts of the colony getting what they wanted while the needs of their district were ignored. All they were asking for was a fair deal. Mr Young was conciliatory but cautioned against mentioning Newcastle as that town had a different set of circumstances. People of the Illawarra believed Newcastle was favoured when it came to government investment. The meeting passed a motion stating that, from an engineering point of view, Port Kembla was the best site and requested an immediate response from the government.[2]

The outcome was favourable, but the building of the deepwater harbour took a while. The announcement of the 1898 *Port Kembla Harbour Act* was just the beginning of the process. Over the next few years land was resumed, jetties built, and with the completion of the eastern breakwater in 1901, ships were finally (if only partially) protected from the regular violent storms. The northern Jetty was not authorised by the State government until 1912. These gales were not ordinary ones. In 1902 the *Sydney Morning Herald* reported:

> On more than one occasion the sea, lashed into fury by a southerly gale, has swept over the breakwater in huge green waves and almost lifted the rails and sleepers on which the locomotive runs, toppled heavy tracks pell mell into the sea and would have swept a workman into the harbour had he not clutched a rope and held on desperately until the wave had passed over him.[3]

## Now a bridge

In the late 1890s the next issue for the town was how to access the port from the land. Tom Thumb Lagoon, the large body of tidal water between Port Kembla and Wollongong, was a barrier. Building a bridge over it became a local priority.

In 1896 people began agitating. They needed a bridge this year, not later, and not a punt as offered by the Minister, Mr Young. It had to be a proper bridge. The people living and working either side of Tom Thumb Lagoon knew that if Newcastle had asked for a bridge it would have been delivered by now. As Mr J Nicholson MP said, 'We contributed a very large amount to the revenue of the country and are not getting our fair share of expenditure.'

They wondered what it would take to get the politicians' attention and to encourage them to open their pockets. On Thursday 6 August a large South Coast delegation arrived in force for a meeting in Wollongong with the Minister for Public Works, Mr Young, to put their case for the bridge. Mr Alexander Campbell argued that 'the request was not made as a favour but as a public right'. They were sure the Minister would see it their way once he understood. No, a punt was no use, the tides were uncertain, the mayor, Mr Beetson, had surely explained that clearly enough.

A bridge over Allans Creek didn't serve their purposes. It was too far to the west. And what about the coal-trimmers? These low-paid men shovelled coal into coal boilers on the ships, making sure it was evenly 'trimmed' or balanced in the bunkers so the ship wasn't lopsided, and came backwards and forwards twice a day, wading through neck-deep water, dealing with tricky tides and the possibility of sharks. Imagine doing the journey during inclement weather; it was 'cruel and barbarous', according to one delegate. Men had been known to get cramps in winter and give up their work because of the hardship. And what about Mr Weeks? He'd nearly lost his life while crossing the lagoon – on several occasions his horse and cart were almost swept away.

On and on they went. Other merchants were sick of their sulkies getting bogged in the mud. It was economic suicide for the district, boats were known to fill up with provisions at other ports because of the inconvenience. Passengers couldn't disembark and do some touring and as for the sailors, their social needs were not being met. The *Illawarra Mercury* reported a resident saying, 'Nature had designed Port Kembla for a harbour and with a little assistance it could be converted into one of the best in the world.' The barrage of complaint worked. They'd come out in force to confront the Minister and partially got what they wanted.[4]

The first pile for the bridge was sunk in 1889 and the government was fortunate as it was mostly built by volunteers. They found their own rough bush timber and constructed a one-metre wide bridge which was finished in 1896 and called Trimmers Bridge. It was a vast improvement. Men no longer waded through swirling tidal water or travelled by flat-bottom punt. However, it was not until 1910 that the Department of Main Roads built a road bridge, just west of Trimmers Bridge.

From 1910 to 1955 this bridge connected Port Kembla people to the outside world.

The bridge played an important part in my family's life and featured in many of my mother's childhood stories. From 1910 onwards our family trotted over it in sulkies, horse-drawn coaches, double-decker buses and, later, our Morris Oxford. I still recall my journeys; the sound of the clickety-clack of the wooden planks, low over the water, being enveloped by sea, sky and the smell of salty air. In 1955 when I was 12 the bridge closed and work began on the inner harbour – a change so rapid that an important part of my family's geographical remembering disappeared.

# 6
# Nothing's stopping them

Entrepreneurial white men of the early twentieth century saw a chance for development in Port Kembla and took it. The raw materials were at hand, a port was created and the original inhabitants were swept aside. Considering the combination of time, place and economic circumstances, the establishment of heavy industry was inevitable. Workers were soon on their way and building houses to live in. A reticulated water supply brought fresh water from Cordeaux Dam, and the trappings of town life quickly followed. Life was energetic: sailors came and went, industries started up, buildings of every kind appeared and shops opened. My mother Audrey remembers:

> The breakwaters were built from great pieces of stone quarried about a mile from our house. It passed by on flat-topped rail cars to the site. As the breakwaters grew they became favourite walking places for courting couples on Sundays and holidays. When we had to dodge waves because of rough seas it added to the fun.

I look for evidence of my family in the rush to create this town. The earliest buildings in Port Kembla and all over Australia were often churches. They went up fast, providing meeting places for all denominations: Catholic, Methodist, Anglican, Presbyterian. Searching for evidence of my grandparents, Alfred and Gertrude, led me to a 1911 newspaper report in the *South Coast Times* where I find their names:

> On Sunday last the new Methodist Church at Port Kembla opened for service. The pulpit was occupied by the Rev. CT Newman. The weather was threatening and the services were not as well attended as expected.[1]

A description of the church concert held on the previous Wednesday followed and like many occasions of the time, it had several purposes: part business meeting and part social event. It began with 'a very nice tea provided by the ladies' then on to business: debts incurred in creating of the church for building, furniture and an organ. The cut-price on the organ, if paid off quickly, was discussed. Fencing was mentioned and plans made to get that done. As horses like Darcy were wandering around eating what they liked, this made sense. Benefactors were named and thanked, including Alfred Hartley, my grandfather, who contributed ten shillings and sixpence – this was generous. According to the New South Wales Industrial Court in 1914, a living wage for a family of four was 48 shillings per week ($232).[2]

The Glen Airlie Quartet sang 'Who's Catching Fish?' and were 'heartily recalled'. Miss Gibson of Wollongong, 'a very young lady with a pleasing voice', sang two solos. Mr Wiseman, not to be outdone, sang 'Open the Gates Triumphant' and 'Off to Philadelphia in the Morning', 'getting for the latter an insistent recall'. Three others sang before Mr Willsmore 'entertained the audience immensely' with 'Uncle Podger Hanging a Picture'. Mr Broomfield's display of 'clever balance juggling' which finished the night was no anticlimax.

I admire these talented amateurs, happy to perform in public, remembering their words and music and entertaining the people in the church that Wednesday night in 1911. The mix of jam sponges, singing, recitation and juggling appeals to me. The building of a church and raising the money was free-spirited. Today there would be regulations, workplace agreements and a hundred and one bits of paperwork. Life seemed more spontaneous then. I remember this church and was sad not to find it when I returned recently. As a family we visited it on alternate Sundays. My father saw himself as a Methodist and my mother, an Anglican. I went along as a child but preferred the Anglican St Stephen's with its stained-glass windows and more theatrical services.

## A two-storey school

Six years and three temporary buildings later, Port Kembla got the school it wanted at the top of the hill on Military Road opposite St Stephens. A member of my family saved a photo of the opening. Bunting decked the severe building, giving it a half-hearted celebratory look. It was more like an orphanage from the nineteenth century than a modern school of 1917. At the time reports were enthusiastic. The *South Coast Times* called the opening 'a red letter day for the Port', and believed the building would stand as 'an everlasting monument' to the enterprise of the Progress Association, the parents and the public generally. A program of events was organised to mark the day. From 11 a.m. the children were entertained at a sports picnic. There were races for valuable prizes and the ladies made sure 'hundreds of healthy little appetites were fully satisfied'. HR Lee was responsible for driving the school project. This comes as no surprise after researching Port Kembla's history – he is continually mentioned. Locals expecting something special on the day of the opening were not disappointed.

The formal part of proceedings was begun by the children 'lustily singing' 'Advance Australia Fair'. There were bands, supplemented from Wollongong, and speeches. Mr James, the Minister for Education, declared the school open by turning a silver key in the lock. The key had been made by men at ER&S from electrolytic silver. 'It was more than a memento ... it was a reminder of what could be accomplished in the Port Kembla district,' Mr James enthused. Bouquets were given to politicians' wives, and the new Beale piano (the same make as my grandparents'), which had arrived that morning, was admired.[3] All my family went to this school: my uncles, my aunt, my mother and me.

## A picture theatre

Going to the movies was the ultimate treat for a child, as it was for the rest of the town's residents. The film craze began early. After several attempts at showing movies in the Empire Hall, the Port Kembla Amusement Company was formed by certain businessmen, including HR Lee, and purchased a site in 1914 and built a weatherboard structure 30 feet by 70 feet (9 by 21 metres). There were film screenings on alternate nights, as well as bazaars, concerts, dances and other social functions. Unsuccessful years followed before Mr Robert Shipp took over the lease, then bought the freehold, and called it the Empire Picture Show. However, it wasn't until the late 1920s that he fulfilled his grand dream by building the Whiteway Theatre on the same site in Wentworth Street. He modelled it on the Rialto Theatre in Manly. Economic reality prevailed and the grander features of the Rialto, such as its state-of-the-art ventilation and four-piece orchestra, were not included.

Initially there was only enough electricity for lighting, so the projector had to be turned by hand, resulting in pauses at the end of each reel as the next one was threaded. This happened often. The projection box, resembling a tool box, was suspended eight feet (2.4 metres) above the floor and the fire risk, by today's standards, was unthinkable. Showing films at the Whiteway was an ad hoc kind of business as the *South Coast Times* reported in September 1951:

> The original recording of talkie films was done on slow speed discs and synchronised with a silent

> film. It is not hard to imagine the chaos when, as in the case of 'Madame X', the recorded reports of gun shots bounced the turntable arm out of its correct grove into another. The effect was that the guns did the dialogue and the players 'spoke' the gun shots. It is little wonder that high blood pressure was the prevailing ill of early showmen.[4]

But nobody worried about the less-than-perfect moments, the hard seats, the fire risks or the flickering images – Hollywood had come to town: *Broadway Melody* in 1930, *Mutiny on the Bounty* in 1935 and *The Great Ziegfeld* in 1936. Admission prices were sixpence and ninepence, rising to one shilling, and later to one shilling and sixpence. In 1929 the first talking film was shown, *The Black Watch* with Myrna Loy and Victor McLaglen – a cathartic mix of epic adventure and a hero's moral fibre being tested in exotic India.

## A town with all mod cons

All this was achieved in the first decades of the twentieth century – not bad if you ignored who was displaced, the effect development had on the natural environment, and the price paid by many workers with their lives. The tone of the following extract from the *Illawarra Mercury* of Friday 2 January 1920 interests me. People responded to events with a detached, matter-of-fact calmness.

## PORT KEMBLA NEWS

## THE STRIKE

The hum of industry is conspicuous by its absence at both the E. R. and S. Co. and M. M. Coy's works owing to the strike. Though a fortnight has elapsed since the men ceased work, no settlement of the dispute is yet in sight, and a protracted struggle seems inevitable. No further developments have taken place on either side, though rumour is prevalent that the E. R. & S. Works are shortly to close down for some months. At the present time only sufficient power is being generated by members of the staff to maintain the electric lighting system. To relieve the stress of unemployment, the strikers are engaging in fishing, prawning, and rabbiting.

A meeting of members of the A.W.U. employed at the E. R. & S. Works was held on Saturday, 20th, Mr. Geo. Keen presiding. Business relating to the men off work was discussed, but no finality was arrived at as a result of the meeting.

## ACCIDENT

A painful accident befell Mr G. Simon at the E.R. & S. Works on Friday night, when he was jammed between two skips in the boiler house.

He sustained internal injuries, which necessitated his laying up for several days.

## THUNDERSTORM

A thunderstorm, accompanied by vivid flashes of lightning and deafening roars of thunder, swept over the township on Wednesday morning. Several persons were badly frightened, and the gatehouse keeper at the Electrolytical Works had an unpleasant shock through fusing of the telephone wires.

## OVER THE BREAKWATER

Small hope is entertained of being able to salvage the locomotive which recently plunged over the breakwater. Despite many efforts to recover the engine, it gradually settled down and now lies at a depth of 90 feet. Reviewing the simplicity with which the accident happened, the marvel is that the driver did not find a watery grave. It appears that the engine power was being used, in conjunction with a large pole, to force a boulder over the breakwater when the pole broke. The impetus of the locomotive was so great that the driver, being unable to control it, the engine also took the plunge.

A mate probably fished out the locomotive driver, dried him off and he was back driving another locomotive the next day. The people of the Port had decided a laconic sensibility was the best way to respond to the unexpected.

# 7
# Life for the more fortunate, 1910–1930

Some were lucky enough to be on the side of those in charge, the ones with muskets who made the laws and distributed land. Even so, life in early twentieth-century Port Kembla for those lucky ones was not easy. My grandparents lived their lives before cars and electricity. From 1915, they lived with the worry of Audrey's eldest brother, Leigh, fighting in the First World War.

Audrey's diary gives the detail. From 1910 the men of the family were at work in various industries, my grandfather at the copper smelter ER&S, and the women were doing the back-breaking rest. My mother remembers washing day being formidable, even though Queen Rosie was there to help. The copper was lit, clothes scrubbed on a board and hand-wrung. Wooden props, brought from a prop man who came by regularly, held parallel lines of washing which flapped dry above the dusty ground. Sometimes winds brought the lines down and the rinsing and wringing cycle started all over again.

Starching and ironing were next. First the metal irons were heated on the fuel stove and rubbed on a cloth to remove soot. My family presented its face to the world washed, starched and ironed. No wonder they look good in the picnic photos.

Next was shopping at Fairleys in Wentworth Street. It was a structure built of iron with a wooden floor and all goods were carefully displayed. Audrey remembers how 'We would take a jar for honey and fill it from a big tin barrel with a tap.'

Butter and cheese were kept in a fly-proof enclosure and the butter was taken from a large square with butter pats and moulded into shapes and wrapped in greaseproof paper. Everything you could imagine was there. Fowl food was stored in huge bags on the floor. Cooking utensils hung above, and groceries were stacked on shelves. Fishing tackle, sporting gear and gardening supplies were on display. On the other side of the shop were sheets, towels, clothes and shoes for both sexes.

As there was little prepared food for sale, most cooking started from scratch and foraging was part of life. Audrey remembers summer blackberrying expeditions. Gertrude, with family and friends, all in their old clothes, would travel by sulky to Kembla Heights, about 15 kilometres away. After finding the most prolific bushes, Audrey and her siblings were each given a pail and expected to fill it. They returned home, often by moonlight, tired, cut and bitten, with purple stained hands. The rewards were pies, jams and jellies. However, some home cooking Audrey loathed – like the melon and lemon jam that was often cooking on the fuel stove. She was happy most of it was given away to the Red Cross and the church.

I still make Gertrude's Christmas pudding recipe, buying a metre of unbleached calico which I wash and dry. Next I soak a large bowl of dried and glacé fruit in rum for two days. After making a flour, spice, butter and egg batter and incorporating the fruit, I wrap the mixture in calico, tie it with string and boil it for five hours. When I see the round shape hanging on my door knob to dry, I connect to Gertrude.

As I have none of her written words aside from the recipe, I bond through the things she owned. There are a few objects remaining: a silver serviette ring inscribed 'MH', my great-grandmother, Mary Hughson's, initials; a gold bangle; a silver serving dish and cover; a mayonnaise dish, spoon and plate, and a small hand-painted bowl. That's all I have of her material life and I treasure these things. I like the mayonnaise set best with its pale green trim and the spoon with a pansy bud bedded in the bowl. It's whimsical and old fashioned. It came out of the Noritake factory which opened for business in 1904. I don't associate Japanese goods with early Port Kembla but somehow Gertrude acquired it. Worldwide trade was speeding up and goods were flowing and she probably bought it at Lances in Wollongong on one of her shopping trips. This set tells me she loved subtle colours and flowers and liked the ceremony of serving food.

I sometimes wear her gold bangle, shiny and thin from three generations of use. It has a dainty filigree design and a chain keeping it safe. It connects back to a time when women dressed formally and modestly. My mother, influenced by Gertrude's style, worried about modern fashion trends and advised my daughters to 'never lose touch with your femininity'. Gertrude's small flower bowl with its Celtic frieze in muted blues, mauves and oranges has somehow survived. It was made by Annie Buckeridge in 1919 and labelled 'Peace'. This faded, glaze-cracked object, pleasingly tactile, is a physical sample of work by a local artist.

As well as pottery, residents of Port Kembla were busy with other cultural activities.

Music was important to members of my family and, like cooking, it was made at home. My grandfather, born in the 1880s, played a range of instruments and both he and his eldest daughter Hazel were known for their fine voices. They regularly entertained themselves and others around the Beale piano. Leigh's fiancée, Dora Williams, known as Dolly to the family, could sight-read difficult music and in later years, according to Audrey, accompanied Dame Clara Butt at a concert in Brisbane. Dolly was born in Prescot, England, in 1904. How she got to Australia, met my uncle and played for the great contralto is a mystery. 'Land of Hope and Glory' was Clara's signature tune, which she probably sang with stirring gusto while here.

My mother loved music and played both piano and organ. For many years she was part of the life of her church. She knew who had good voices amongst her friends and whether the women were soprano or alto and the men tenor or baritone. They liked gathering around pianos in each other's houses and sang songs with emotionally charged rhythms like 'The Floral Dance', 'The Road to Mandalay' and 'Soldiers of the Queen'.

The dancing words of 'The Floral Dance' were recorded in 1912 by Peter Dawson, the bass baritone from Adelaide. It was one of my father's favourites and when it's played occasionally on radio I stop and remember him.

*We danced to the band with the curious tone*
*Of the cornet, clarinet and big trombone*
*Fiddle, 'cello, big bass drum*
*Bassoon, flute and euphonium*
*Each one making the most of his chance*
*Altogether in the Floral Dance.*

The only alternative to making your own music involved travelling to either Wollongong or Sydney to hear professional musicians. There was no radio until 1923 and the ABC didn't begin broadcasting until 1932. There was intense excitement surrounding the first broadcasts. Every program was live until 1935 and there were no second takes. The ABC became the focus for classical music, appointing Bernard Hinze as musical director and commissioning orchestras in each state. Live concerts were performed and all Shakespeare's 38 plays read between 1936 and 1938. When cricket matches were being played in England, commentators used cables from London and sound effects in the Sydney studio to bring matches alive. Radio for my parents, who were 17 and 18 in 1932, was the equivalent of television for my generation. They infected me with their love for the medium. Summer will always mean the sound of cricket on the radio, the memory of my parents hovering close listening for the rare, dramatic moment in a Test match.

Not only music but timekeeping was an important consideration for my family. Audrey remembers 'A large round alarm clock was our main timepiece, apart from Dad's pocket watch and an old ornamental but inaccurate wall clock.'

Before radio, clocks were of great importance and looked after carefully. In Port Kembla, the ER&S whistle was the town's main source of timekeeping and everyone set their clocks by it. It blew at 7.00 a.m., 7.30 a.m., 3.30 p.m. and 4.00 p.m. and was essential for schools and shift workers. It also sounded for disasters, and workmen and staff would rush to answer its summons.

When my grandfather serviced the family clock it was a complicated procedure. Paper was laid on the table and the clock carefully taken apart. If screws fell on the floor it was a drama and as a child my mother was the one who crawled under the table and found them. A feather was taken from one of the chooks, dipped in oil, and each part of the clock was gently brushed. The whole thing was put back together and time after time the clock ticked on.

Singing around the piano, so important for my grandparents' and parents' social life, waned with daily radio. By the fifties I remember singalongs with the family, but my parents had stopped gathering with their friends to sing and we children had other things on our minds – such as persuading our parents to buy a turntable to play 78 rpm records. We only had one or two records that each played a three- to five-minute song. These we played over and over, singing along with the repetitive words. From my grandparents' lives in the 1900s to the 1960s we lost the art of universal music-making. I learnt piano but my heart wasn't in it. And from the 1930s onwards the hour could be checked by turning on the radio. Technology changed our habits. The whole process has accelerated over the last 60 years and we are now wired for sound, cut off from each other, unaware of what we've lost.

## Fairs and shows

When they weren't making music, the people of Port Kembla were organising events – this was an important part of the town's psyche. With little entertainment available, locals filled the vacuum. By 1921 they were holding their third Poultry and Pigeon Show at the Empire Hall and it was described in detail by the *South Coast Times*.[1] The locals were not put off by unfavourable weather and 'fairly liberal patronage was bestowed'. There were clucking chooks, cooing pigeons, singing canaries and owners and buyers mingling and bargaining. Prizes were awarded for everything: MH Mills won for the best Red Chequer Hen and L Howarth won with his Utility White Leghorn Cock. Pigeon categories depended on the range they could fly, 500 or 250 miles (804 and 402 kilometres respectively). The birds were a serious part of the town's communication system. One group who used them regularly were the coal trimmers working at Port Kembla Harbour. Before the bridge over Tom Thumb Lagoon was built, theirs was an isolating occupation. If they knew they would be working late they sent messages to their families by pigeon with their expected time of return and requests for food. On lonely winter's nights with time to spare, there was a chance for deeply felt thoughts to wing back and forth.

Also at the busy show were mounds of vegetables arranged on trestle tables: squash, rhubarb, parsnips, carrots, radishes and leeks. Cakes were displayed, cooked with eggs from superior poultry: sponge sandwiches, pound cakes, seed cakes and sultana cakes, all asking to be eaten. Bottles of every possible jam were for sale: blackberry, apricot, peach, apple and rhubarb, boiled up by housewives on their Aga stoves. Gardeners were not forgotten, the smell of birds competed with the perfume of flowers: carnations, dahlias, zinnias and chrysanthemums. There were many categories to enter: cut flowers, buttonholes, pot plants and ferns.

All aspects of town life were on show. In 1921 Mr Henry, the headmaster of Port Kembla Public School, marshalled his students to submit displays of their schoolwork. I know my family was involved because the local paper reported that in the section for Australian map drawing, my uncle Harry came second, as he did for chalk drawing. There was a gender divide – girls' names appeared in categories such as 'best-dressed dolly' and 'plain and fancy sewing'. Outside the hall, the Port Kembla Band welcomed show-goers with music, and on the Friday night the committee and judges were entertained to dinner at the Great Eastern Hotel. I imagine my grandparents in the thick of it, enjoying their son Harry's accolades for his map drawing, meeting their friends and checking the goods, and I wonder if Gertrude entered the cake and jam-making competitions. Alfred, a keeper of chooks, surely would have been interested in high-quality egg layers. Local shows provided the perfect barter system – cars had not arrived to break down the reliance on home-made goods.

Early Port Kembla residents organised a town to suit their needs, but the outside world was looming.

# 8
# First World War and aftermath

In 1914 industries and basic services were barely up and running, houses and churches newly built, when an external issue threatened the town's wellbeing – the First World War. My family sent a soldier to the fight, Uncle Leigh. Like many others, he was attracted to a war that promised to test his youthful manliness. Patriotism, loyalty to Britain and a desire for a great adventure inspired Leigh and his friends. Although he suffered from bronchitis, he was determined to enlist. From the long perspective of history it's difficult to understand the war's appeal. Some say it helped shape Australian identity, while others, like historian Peter Stanley, question the Gallipoli myth.

Although she was very young at the time, my mother's childhood memories were dominated by the First World War and fears for her brother's safety. He failed his first medical at 18 due to a chest infection, but his health improved after a year working in Queensland and he was accepted into the Army. He was part of the 7th Field Company Engineers, Reinforcement 3, which left Australia aboard HMAS *Runic* on 20 January 1916. Because of his delayed departure, Leigh missed Gallipoli.

Audrey's strongest memory of those times was Gertrude's anxiety as she read the casualty lists. Leigh kept in touch and sent regular cards. And we have them still: embroidered ones of the Albert (1916) and Verdun (1916) battles in France. They form a special part of our family archive. As a child I viewed them as exotic and admired the beautifully sewn pictures. In the Verdun card, buildings are sewn in grey silk and the fires in shades of pink, with darkest pink reserved for flames escaping through bombed windows. The Verdun battle degenerated into pointless fighting and misplaced prestige and 700,000 men were lost on both sides in ten months. On the sidelines, to mark these catastrophes and make money, local women made card mementos. Young soldiers like Leigh used them to send messages home like this one to his sister Hazel:

> Dear Hazel
>
> Am sending you a couple of pretty cards I noticed in one of the French villages. They are great people for this class of card, but it is very seldom that I come across a decent one when I have got the cash. Either they are too gaudy or the writing is not appropriate. They seem to specialise in 'dear sweetheart, dear wife and dear son and daughter' so of course I can't buy those. Thank you Hazel dear for all those nice letters you write. You are a little bastion, never miss a mail. Irma, Sheila and Mavis have been regular

correspondents lately, Irma also sends The Leader regularly.

Heaps of love and kisses
From
Your loving brother
xxx Leigh

On the back of another card with a picture of a romantic-looking girl holding pine tree branches he wrote:

Dear Audrey

How is the cheeky little kid getting on? I suppose you have grown that much I won't know you when I get back. A big X and tons of love from Leigh.

From 1916 to 1918 my family lived in fear of receiving a telegram with bad news, while trying to live a normal life. What they wanted was detailed news of the war, but this was not easy to come by. Australia's first embedded war journalist, Charles Bean, was hampered by censorship. Historian Ross Coulthart notes the discrepancies between Bean's official reports and his more truthful war diaries in his book *If People Really Knew*. Even if Bean had been honest about the mismanagement of the war, it wouldn't have mattered because by the time his reports were read, the battles were long over. Trawling through Trove, the National Library's online research service, I discovered local newspapers emphasised the successes on our side and used the general word 'enemy' for all nationalities the Australians fought. The following extract, under the headline 'The War', from the *Illawarra Mercury* of 28 September 1917, is an example:

> General Douglas Haig in his latest reports states that after serious fighting all day long the English and Scottish troops ejected the enemy from the position occupied. The enemy developed severe counter attacks but the Australians cleared Polygon Wood and captured a trench system. The enemy losses were heavy. One thousand prisoners were taken.

At this time the town's main focus was supporting their enlisted men in any way they could. It wasn't just the women of France who were busy – Port Kembla's women were brushing up their skills and knitting. Gertrude belonged to the Red Cross and she and other women knitted socks and blankets as well as packing food parcels. At church my grandparents most likely sang the melancholy 'Abide with Me' and the rousing 'Eternal Father, Strong to Save', both popular hymns of the era.

Recruitment marches often passed through town. One of them, the South Coast Waratahs, was led by Captain Blow. It began on 30 November 1915 in Nowra and arrived in Sydney on 18 December. They carried a banner with an embroidered waratah presented to the marchers by the ladies of the Nowra Red Cross. In photographs the men look miserable and badly dressed. Probably news had filtered through that the 'Great Adventure' wasn't so great. Of the 120 men enlisted as a result of this drive, 30 died in the war. Recruiting drives, or snowballing drives as they were called, were later phased out because of low enlistments.

Meanwhile men continued working in the town's industry and everyone waited for news. Although they didn't know it, Port Kembla was on the brink of better times. Its future industrial prosperity was about to be ensured. In 1915 the Australian Commonwealth and State governments cancelled contracts with German copper companies, which provided opportunities for ER&S. But the sticking point was the initial German investment which had helped start the company – no one had worried about this until now, when Germany was the enemy. Once a parcel of shares in the name of the Estate of Siegfried Hirsch was removed, ER&S was ready to benefit. Everyone wanted copper, and so jobs increased, unions formed and the town prospered.

It was a bittersweet boom for many as the war dragged on and fateful telegrams arrived. However, after four years and what must have seemed like an age, the mood lightened. Leigh wrote a postcard to Hazel on 19 July 1918:

> My dear Hazel,
>
> Just a sample of the latest idea in p.c's, 'Silhouettes' they call them.
>
> How are you all out there, still worrying about Fritz's big push I suppose. You want to stop

that. Friend Fritz was never so far from winning as he is now. In fact I wouldn't be surprised to hear the peace bells ringing in the near future.
Love to you all

from Your loving brother
xxxx Leigh

On 11 November 1918 the Armistice between the Western Allies and Germany was signed, and after another six months, peace terms were struck at the Treaty of Versailles. Leigh was not repatriated until April 1919, as it wasn't easy finding ships to bring all the men home. As news of Leigh's imminent arrival filtered through, the family began preparing, along with other families of returning soldiers. When the steam train drew into Wollongong station, bands played and banners decorated the streets. Mayors made speeches and mothers hugged their sons very close, amazed at their good fortune. Audrey remembers helping decorate their house with steamers in preparation for Leigh's homecoming, being picked up and hugged by a strange brother at the station and travelling home for the celebratory feast.

The age of naivety was over. One in five who left to fight did not return: 60,000 of them. One in three who did return were incapacitated in some way. With a bit of luck, like Leigh had, you came home. His chest condition had prevented him joining up earlier and saved him from Gallipoli, and somehow he had survived the rest of the carnage, though he suffered from the after-effects of gas attacks. Even for the 'lucky' ones it wasn't easy. They returned, heads filled with battle images, suffering from physical injuries and facing uncertain economic futures. As early as 1916 Vincent Borbham was bemoaning the disorganised approach taken to helping returned men and women:

> An appeal has been sent out this week under the authority of the RSA (Returned Servicemen's Association) for funds to assist returned men who are at this season of the year without means, many of whom are married men with children. Is it not a scandalous state of affairs that this is so? Hundreds of pounds are lying idle somewhere and everyone is asking what has become of them.[1]

Compounding the situation, on the soldiers' return an influenza epidemic broke out. It killed 40–60 million people around the world, many more than in the First World War and beyond any other catastrophic event in history. This event seems to have slipped from our global collective memory. At the time, like the rest of Australia, everyone on the South Coast was apprehensive and there was disappointment – soldiers were returning and everyone wanted to celebrate. Authorities put off the official Illawarra Armistice Day celebrations for six months because of the flu scare. Even the 1919 Wollongong Show was postponed, a highlight of the year for many, including Audrey. The focus was on the emergency. An inoculation centre was established at the Wollongong Town Hall and the Wollongong

Infants School was turned into a temporary isolation ward. People travelling further south than Dapto, only a few kilometres from Wollongong, needed authorisation papers, and on buses everyone wore face masks. In February 1919, demonstrating how on edge the district was, a steamer arriving to load coal in Port Kembla Harbour with a sailor on board with flu, was immediately ordered into quarantine.

Without modern medical knowledge the community was ill-equipped to manage the epidemic. We know now that viruses cause flu, not bacteria as was thought at the time, and the inoculations handed out did nothing to protect people. The only result was probably a lessening of secondary bacterial infections. It was not until 1930 that researchers discovered viruses caused influenza and not until the 1940s that antibiotics were readily available to treat bacterial infections. The mood in town at the time was ominous. Audrey remembers yellow flags tied on the gates of houses in Port Kembla to warn of infection. A large horse-drawn dray filled by ER&S with blankets, soup and other food made deliveries every day to stricken families. Her family was infected but all survived. The events of the first two decades of the twentieth century left their mark on her.

# 9
# Audrey

Although Audrey was a child during the First World War, a teenager during the Great Depression and a young married woman during the Second World War, she was full of fun. These events taught her resilience and may also have been the reason she liked dressing up and pretty things. She was the youngest child by five years and spent a lot of time at home with her father. Her mother, Gertrude, now in her forties, was out and about enjoying town life. When Alfred wasn't working he was happy staying at home, using little Audrey as his excuse. They shared a similar sense of humour, told each other stories and played cards.

When she started school in 1919 her elder brother and sister were already at work. As the youngest, and fussed-over child, school came as a shock. Each day she walked from Darcy Road up the hill past ER&S to the Port Kembla Public School, which by then was located at the top of Military Road. Her beloved brother, Harry, who was five years older, walked with her. According to Audrey the best thing about school was reading, and she was happy in Fifth and Sixth Class when she was allowed to use the library. She disliked some of the teachers because they were often sarcastic, and she was afraid of getting the cane, though she never did.

Her standout memory from childhood was the Wollongong Show, especially the fairy floss and kewpie dolls on sticks. Journeys by horse-drawn public coach to stay with her third cousins, the McPhees, in Wollongong were another highlight.

> The visits, usually three days, were wonderful – they were such interesting children, there were six of them, and we played engrossing games. The only drawback was watching their greatly bearded grandfather eat.

She preferred high school in Wollongong to primary school, and loved reading poetry. On one occasion she remembers being taken to see a Shakespearean play in Sydney. She enjoyed French, her first introduction to a foreign language, and history, especially Ancient History. She remembers teachers for different reasons, liking Miss Doubleday, the assistant head, because of the way she spoke and the way she dressed in different coloured silk blouses. An economics teacher challenged her by saying, 'Everyone should take a turn at picking up the garbage.' However, there was a maths teacher who didn't impress because he didn't try, and some women teachers had trouble disciplining students. She remembers the day a mouse was put in a teacher's desk.

She didn't complete the Leaving Certificate (the equivalent of the Higher School Certificate), leaving school after Fourth

Year, aged 16. Doing this extra year was unusual – most of her peers left after Third Year. She was often sick with bronchitis and missed weeks of school. And getting there was an effort: it was a mile (1.6 kilometre) walk to the train each morning in Port Kembla and then two miles' walk in Wollongong plus the return trip in the afternoon. She remembers being good at basketball and one time after she had been away for six weeks with pneumonia she returned to find they'd kept two positions open for her: she could be in the 'A' team or captain of the 'Bs'. She chose the latter. After school she went to secretarial college in Wollongong, and later worked as a secretary at ER&S. As a child I was aware of my mother's love of reading and sensed her frustration at not being able to continue her education.

While Audrey was going to school, her siblings were meeting partners, getting married and having babies. In 1924, when Audrey was ten, Hazel, her older sister by 13 years, was married. She adored Hazel and I absorbed my mother's love of her. Through my childhood, my connection with Hazel was via birthday parcels sent every year from England. By the time they reached Australia the contents were falling out of their brown paper wrappings. Inside each parcel were magical things, not valuable but special in some way, and a card with words written as if she knew me, although we had never met. Growing up, Audrey thought Hazel was perfect: she was easygoing, had a beautiful singing voice, a sense of humour and a gift for organising picnics and parties. At home with the Hartleys was a fun place to be – by the time Audrey was five, Hazel was hitting her stride.

Somewhere Hazel met an Englishman, Frank Dowley, and married him at St Stephen's Port Kembla on 14 June 1924. Without the 20 June copy of the *Illawarra Mercury* I'd have nothing to go by. She's called 'a remarkably popular and charming girl' and her dress is described in detail: 'ivory satin mousseline, with draped skirt and shirred bodice, finished at the waist with silver tissue and satin cabochon'. She carried a bouquet of white roses and pink sweet peas and was accompanied by little sister Audrey as bridesmaid, who wore a 'dainty frock of pale pink crepe de chine and a black velvet hat trimmed with hand-made flowers and carrying a bouquet of pale pink sweet peas.' It seems miraculous that these first-hand details have survived. Through them I sense the importance of the event for the family. Her father, Alfred, gave her away; big brother Leigh was best man; and ten-year-old Audrey was loving the party atmosphere and feeling special as her sister's only bridesmaid. I'm amazed at the sophistication of the dressing. Who had the expertise to whip up frocks in mousseline satin with cabochon trim in Port Kembla in the 1920s?

Frank and Hazel moved to Sydney and a year later identical twins May and June were born. The girls were knitting-pattern-book babies, almost too beautiful to be believed. Audrey and her mother Gertrude adored them. However, the tight-knit family was about to be broken up as Frank decided to return to England with his family. They went by ship, taking six months, and Hazel never saw her parents again. It would be 40 years before she reconnected with her sister and met me. Port Kembla has always been a place where people came for a generation or two and then moved on.

# 10
# Boom times

History didn't intend Port Kembla to be a slumbering seaside fishing and farming town. Its confluence of sheltered deepwater harbour and supplies of high-quality coking coal drew one industry after another. People came from all parts of Australia – and later the world – to work at Port Kembla. Both my father and grandfather came because of the work on offer. It's hard for me to accept, but if iron smelting and steel production hadn't begun in the town, I wouldn't exist. As I recoiled from everything to do with heavy industry as a teenager, this comes as a shock. Captain Cook's Red Point was renamed Port Kembla because of the coal shipped from the Mount Kembla mine on the escarpment. The Aboriginal meaning of 'kembla' is 'plenty of game' and for white male industrialists that was true, though instead of hunting birds to eat they made steel, copper and fertilisers.

Port Kembla became an exhilarating melting pot because of this upturn in activity. Its harbour was chosen to develop instead of Wollongong, and four breakwaters were built in ten years from 1898 to 1908. Heavy industry started with coke ovens built by the Mount Lyell company in 1899, next to the Mount Kembla Colliery jetty. When the road bridge over the entrance to Tom Thumb Lagoon was later constructed, traffic flowed between Port Kembla and Wollongong. The trifecta of ER&S, Metal Manufactures and Australian Fertilisers brought employment, prosperity and putrid air to Port Kembla for many years to come. The leviathan of them all was the Steelworks, brought to town by the Hoskins family.

Sheila Hoskins, daughter-in-law of Cecil, showed me an 1874 etching of Tom Thumb Lagoon bought by her husband at a London auction. A lone Aboriginal man is standing, spear poised, looking at an expanse of water surrounded by hills. The land surrounding the lagoon later became the site for the Hoskins Steelworks.

The etching shocks with its pristine beauty. As a child travelling by bus on the bridge over Tom Thumb Lagoon, I would imagine Matthew Flinders and George Bass in the area seeing activity which had been undisturbed for centuries: the local men fishing or hunting for wildfowl, the women busy with fires, collecting food, and family matters, chattering together while children swam or slid down sand hills, naked and happy. The navigators, with a sweep of the eye, saw all this plus wooded hills, water, sand and sky beyond. Today, the lagoon depicted in the etching is a busy working inner harbour, and as I stand watching the huge ships move into place, I think of the original people.

In 1816, without consulting these inhabitants or considering their rights for compensation, the area encompassing present-day Port Kembla was granted to the newly arrived Deputy Commissary General, David Allan. He swapped his 2200 acres in Upper Minto for the same amount in the Illawarra. He was a man known for shady deals who earned the suspicion of Governor Macquarie and was moved in 1822 to Barbados. In 1828 he did very well out of the sale of Illawarra Farm when he sold it to Richard Jones for £1617. A year later William Charles Wentworth, the famous explorer and politician, acquired the property and renamed it Five Islands Estate. A caveat was put on the land that it was not to be sold for 21 years after his death, which occurred in 1872. His son Darcy leased the land to various people, including 30 acres to Mount Kembla Coal in 1882.[1]

## The steel story begins

In 1921 the saga of Australia's largest steelworks began when William Charles Wentworth, a descendant of the explorer, sold 400 acres of the Five Islands Estate to Charles Hoskins and his son Cecil. A landscape of inlets and rolling hills was about to be transformed into a massive steelmaking operation.

The history of steelmaking in Port Kembla began many years before, in 1896, when Charles and George Hoskins, sons of an immigrant gunsmith, established a small engineering workshop in Sydney. After modest success, a move to larger premises and a government contract to lay pipes for Sydney's water supply, they were on their way. A branch opened in Melbourne in 1890, and the laying of pipes to supply water from Perth to Coolgardie led Charles to think about the business's dependence on raw materials from overseas. Over the next 20 years Charles took over the ironworks in Lithgow, moved his family there and brought out his brother George. He was an imperious, impatient protectionist and no friend of unions, but this was the man who established Hoskins Iron and Steel in 1919.

When Charles and his son Cecil realised the difficulties of making steel in Lithgow, distant from raw materials except for coal, they turned to Port Kembla. Iron ore, limestone and coal are needed to make steel, as well as a port to ship in raw materials and ship out the finished product. With coal mines nearby, limestone deposits easily accessible and a harbour, Port Kembla was an ideal site. The iron ore came from Port Pirie in South Australia. When they announced their decision to move to the town, the *Sydney Morning Herald* reported the area's reaction:

> The definite announcement by Mr Charles Hoskins and Messrs G. and C. Hoskins had [*sic*] decided to erect steelworks at Port Kembla has caused widespread satisfaction throughout the district.[2]

Not only Port Kembla was in love with steel. In country Moree, journalists waxed lyrical about the stuff. This extract from an article in the *North West Champion* was published under the headline, 'The World Pulsates to the Clamour for Steel':

> The world is calling for steel, the cables tell us every day – steel for warships and merchant men, for canon and plough shares, for forts and skyscrapers, for tanks and motor cars. There is scarcely a thing in the world we can less afford to be without at peace and war. Steel dominates the industrial world as cotton did a century ago, but with ten times the power, and a hundred times the possibilities.[3]

As Moree was the centre of cotton growing, this was a generous evaluation of the changed fortunes of their product versus steel. Country-wide, steel was seen as the next big thing. With the blowing of the first blast furnace at Port Kembla on 29 August 1928, everyone celebrated the start of steelmaking and future prosperity.

But not so fast – decisions made in faraway boardrooms would affect many towns like Port Kembla around the world.

11

# 1930s: Depression and beyond

My mother remembers men out of work, hungry and desperate. They gathered in the streets, and many came to the Hartley kitchen door where Gertrude, my grandmother, always had food for them. My family was lucky; my grandfather Alfred had a job throughout the Depression as an accountant at ER&S, and a company house came with the job, but good fortune was not taken for granted. It had a lasting effect on my mother's generation. She and my father were thrifty recyclers who bought only what they could afford – except for the occasional hat which my mother couldn't resist.

During the Depression the town felt ad hoc and temporary – men who had come searching for work were often forced to live in shanty settlements and camps in Flinders Street and other cheap rental sites. Over the next decade there were constant calls for a permanent solution. The *Sydney Morning Herald* noted:

> … ten per cent of the population of Port Kembla live in bark or bag shanties and some houses are

> grossly overcrowded. Even if there should be no increase in the number of men employed at Port Kembla, it will be five years, at the present state of building before homes can be provided for the men employed in the town.[1]

In 1944 the problem still existed and people were dying because of it. Under the headline, 'Port Kembla Homes Criticised', the *Sydney Morning Herald* reported:

> … after the death of John Roach in a fire in the so-called temporary settlement in Port Kembla, Mr Musgrove the coroner noted that the houses in the settlement are built of weatherboard and canvas with an iron roof and consist of three rooms. They were built during the Depression as a temporary measure but, because of the shortage of proper housing they had become more or less permanent.[2]

Politicians could not agree on how to solve the issue. On Tuesday 24 August 1931 Mr Bert Lazzarini MHR came to town and addressed a meeting for an hour in the Memorial Hall. He believed the industrial system was broken and that the Federal government under prime ministers Bruce and Page had borrowed too much and spent too lavishly. He wanted a 'scheme of aggressive national works' using a form of Commonwealth notes for the payment of wages. He was against 'The Australian Premiers Plan' which suggested cutting spending. He supported the Lang Plan of building public works. However, after the December 1931 elections Jack Lang was no longer Premier of New South Wales and the plan came to nothing.[3]

Port Kembla's industry was also affected. With peace, the demand for copper had plummeted. Between 1918 and 1921 Australian copper ore output fell by more than 70 per cent. Because ER&S was next door to Metal Manufactures it was able to maintain its position as the largest copper smelter and refinery in the British Empire. But production never equalled the 1918 peak of 36,480 tons. Steelmaking also had problems because of lack of funds. In an attempt to raise revenue, in 1926 Hoskins Iron and Steel changed its name to Australian Iron and Steel (AIS) and issued 300,000 preference shares. But without the capital to finalise the transfer from Lithgow of all the equipment necessary for a viable steelmaking process, including the building of an open-hearth furnace, the company remained vulnerable. Broken Hill Propriety Ltd (BHP) exploited its difficulties and was happy to accept AIS's offer of a merger in 1935. Now BHP controlled steelmaking in both Newcastle and Port Kembla and AIS, the Hoskins' grand dream, was reduced to a subsidiary.

***

Although the 1930s were tough for many, good things did happen in the town, such as the celebrations marking the opening of the extensions to the Port Kembla School. The *Illawarra Mercury* reported that guests were greeted by 'a posse of welcome' from boy scouts with District Commissioner CFT Jackson in charge.4 Mr William Davies, the New South Wales Minister of Education, spoke at length, and students performed. First they sang the national anthem, followed by 'Australia's Sunny Clime'. There was more: a character sketch, 'The Knife'; a recitation of 'The Bush School'; dancing of the Highland Fling and finally a scene, 'The Railway Porter'. Mr Davies was presented with a Port Kembla-made copper key and used it to open the door to the new wing. After an inspection of the new space and distribution of bouquets to dignitaries' wives, afternoon tea was served by the ladies of the Parents and Citizens Association.

If there was nothing else to do you could always go to the Whiteway – that's if you could afford it. Members of my family were probably at the 2 p.m. Saturday matinee on Saturday, 16 January 1932, to see Will Rogers in *Ambassador Bill* and James Dunn in *Sob Sister*. The operators knew what the town liked, screening Don Bradman playing in the Third Test Match and Mickey Mouse in *The Birthday Party*. Two films, a newsreel and a cartoon – all included in the price of a ticket.

The opening of the Moss Vale to Port Kembla railway line was another event which provided distraction. This occurred on Saturday, 20 August 1932, and created a link between the coastal town and the Southern Highlands. The newspapers at the time captured the excitement, describing how the Premier of New South Wales, Mr Bertram Stevens, cut the ribbon amid 'stirring scenes of enthusiasm'. The first train was packed with 1,000 residents from the Highlands and flags fluttered from schools, halls and railway stations along the route. Scout bands, mobilised by the ubiquitous Charles Jackson, played as the train arrived at Unanderra, the station on the southern side of Port Kembla. The reporter from the *South Coast Times* called it a 'perfect day that seemed to be Nature's blessing on the animated and important proceedings'. The whole enterprise was begun when Charles Hoskins promised that if a railway line was built his company would establish a steelworks in Port Kembla. There were limestone mines at Marulan near Goulburn and a railway line from Moss Vale would facilitate the transporting of limestone. The Department of Public Works took the bait and began investigating. Nine years and one and half million pounds later it was done.

However, what really caught the imagination of the locals at this time was the opening of the Port Kembla Baths in 1937. No one worried about the cost of £16,500. The *South Coast Times* described the opening as a 'gala day' – no wonder, as 4,000 came to enjoy the event. Everyone heralded the new pool as a symbol of the prosperity hovering in the air. Mr Eric Spooner, Minister for Local Government and Public Works, did the honours. He must have liked opening swimming pools as later in the year he cut the ribbon at the King George V Memorial Park Olympic pool in Forbes. Multi-tasking Mr Spooner not only officiated but found time to design a neck-to-knee swimming costume for the Port Kembla Show, called the 'Spooner Costume'. Made of wool, in hot weather it drove those with sensitive skins mad with the itch. Mr Spooner was very happy with his creation because of its supreme modesty and came to consider it one of his career highlights. His daughter, Lesley Hordern, edited and published his diary in 2001: *The Man who Designed a Bathing Costume.* During the opening of the pool Mr Spooner anticipated that the baths were here to meet the requirements of a large city that would some day be established. The future of Port Kembla was no longer a vision but a reality – it was already the third manufacturing centre of New South Wales and promised to become the third city of New South Wales.[5]

Everyone was talking up the fortunes of the town. Mr Graham Matthews, the president of the Shire of the Central Illawarra, enthused about the growing diversity of trade at the port and, warming to the topic, reeled off future projects: the extension to the Northern Breakwater, the reconstruction of No. 3 Wharf into a low-level wharf capable of handling coke as well as coal, a rail connection and a fitted travelling crane.

More followed: Mr Spooner cut the ribbon, followed by a diving exhibition, clowns, and two bands belting out their favourite tunes. Afternoon tea was served in a marquee where Mr Spooner was presented with a souvenir program bound in Moroccan leather. Mr Gorrell was the first councillor to swim in the pool and, exhilarated by the experience, he said, 'Every man woman and child should lift their hats to him [Mr Spooner].' Port Kembla was going to be a city and nothing could hold it back.

The locals had built the baths, many while on

unemployment relief during the Depression, and they celebrated in their own way. A wheelbarrow race was held from Tom Thumb Bridge to Allan Street, a scooter race from Port Kembla Post Office to the baths, and there was a bicycle race and a boxing tournament. The people of the town had a reputation for organising entertainment and they weren't going to disappoint.[6]

I like the way Port Kembla did things. Yes, there were the usual bureaucrats and speeches, but also a crazy mix of entertainment – there was a sense of fun, with anarchic clowns often blurring boundaries at official openings. Port Kembla people didn't take themselves too seriously. As part of the sporting events scheduled for the baths' opening, men, 18 of them according to *South Coast Times*, pushed wheelbarrows all the way from Tom Thumb Bridge to Allan Street. Mr Martin from Crown Street, Wollongong, was declared the winner, 200 yards (182 metres) ahead of Mr Puckeridge of Bland Street, Port Kembla, in second place.[7]

My father arrived in Port Kembla at this time and met my mother. The opening of the baths and similar events encouraged them and others to see a bright future in the town.

Audrey and Doug, the day they bought the engagement ring, 1938

12

# Audrey and Doug

They look right together in this photograph, holding hands and dressed up for ring buying. Doug, proud in his three-piece suit, and Audrey, slim, elegant and striding in perfect step, is saying something with that jaunty hat. They went to Sydney to do their shopping. I wonder why Doug is carrying a case – is it full of cash to pay for the ring?

It was almost inevitable, Doug ending up in Port Kembla. Work opportunities in Adelaide where he was born were few, and with his new metallurgical qualifications and the expansion of Port Kembla's fledgling Steelworks there were opportunities for him here. Once he arrived everything fell quickly into place. My father was a good-looking man: he smoked a pipe, rode a motorbike, had slicked back hair, grew a moustache and wore clothes with panache. My mother liked to tell stories of young men arriving by train in the mid-1930s. They came with their new degrees lured by almost certain work at the Hoskins Steelworks, recently bought by BHP. Mrs Chapman ran a boarding house in Port Kembla and that's where the men mostly lived. My father had a letter of introduction to the Pratt family, who happened to be the parents of my mother's best friend, Jean. Mr Pratt held Friday night poker sessions to which the recently arrived young men were invited.

With the town full of eligible young men there were many reasons to organise tennis parties, picnics and singalongs. Cute little Audrey, only 157.5 centimetres, who loved pretty clothes until the very end (she never wore trousers), was one of the first to suggest dances at any one of the available halls in Port Kembla, at Marshall Mount and even on Gooseberry Island in the middle of Lake Illawarra. Dressed up and flirting, they'd do the jitterbug and charleston, pairing off into lifetime relationships. Somewhere in the social whirl my parents made up their minds. My father proposed at Minnamurra Falls (where my husband John proposed to me, 28 years later) and they were married in March 1939. Doug was 24 and Audrey 25.

My father grew up in Woodville, South Australia. He was clever, topping primary school and sitting his Leaving Certificate a year early, coming sixth in the state in chemistry. Physics was his favourite subject, but he left the practical book at home and was half an hour late for the exam. He wanted to study engineering at university, but with four siblings and a youngest sister at a private school, there was insufficient money for that, so he went to the School of Mines instead. The school was established in 1886 for technical and practical instruction in engineering, mining, agriculture and other industries. The building is still there on Adelaide's North Terrace near

Parliament House and is now part of the University of Adelaide. His grandfather, David Nock, who had been a member of parliament, was a philanthropic wowser of a Methodist. He introduced a bill calling for six o'clock closing which was passed in October 1877 and became known as Nock's Act. Doug didn't say how he felt about growing up in Adelaide, all I know is that he couldn't wait to leave. When I was a child my mother wrote the weekly letters to his mother, Elsie. My father added *and Doug* at the bottom of the last page in his spidery writing.

Audrey and Doug's marriage was a success. She was gregarious, full of fun and inherited her mother's cooking skills. He worked hard, built a house and adored her, not that he liked to share. I was careful, once he was home for the night, not to monopolise her attention. I was often the only child there. Monday to Friday, from the ages of six to 16, my brother David was at the School for the Deaf in Sydney. My perception of my father is tested by an old newspaper report I found in the *South Coast Times*:

> Fourteen Apexians attired as Chinese presented a delightful floor show at the Apex ball at the RSL on June 4th. 14 men fluttered their fans and did a dance to the strains of Mr Ching Chong and Chinee Girl. The crowd was even more enthusiastic when the dancers for an encore gave a display of tumbling.[1]

My father's name, Doug Nock, is listed among the performers. I'm amazed – he is the last person I would associate with this sort of activity, which shows how little I really knew him. I remember dressing up in the outfit for years: the hat with its black pigtail and the silky pyjamas and top. One night, at the wedding of a daughter of a family friend, I remember seeing him in white shirt and tails, debonair and ebullient. I always understood he was a man's man and reinvented himself at parties.

## March 1939, the Nock–Hartley wedding

Although it was raining and her parents were absent due to ill health, Audrey and Doug's wedding was celebrated. I'm lucky to know this because of a faded newspaper clipping which Audrey saved. A reporter from the *Illawarra Mercury* was there.[2] Dahlias decorated the church, and Audrey's magnolia satin dress was shirred at the waist with the skirt ending in a sweep of train. The long veil of hand-embossed net was held in place by gardenias and she carried white gladioli and tuber roses. Her bridesmaid, Norma Breeze, wore a dress of blue cobweb lace mounted on satin with a halo hat to match. Mrs Day played the organ and, as a tribute to Audrey, who was also an organist at the church, the full choir sang with Effie Simmonds as soloist. Harry, her brother, gave her away and held a wedding reception at his house in Bland Street with his wife, Ella. Rex, my father's older brother, was best man and my father's mother Elsie was there, wearing a dress of mulberry silk, but not her husband.

I wonder why not. When she left the reception, Audrey wore a powder blue romaine 'frock' (never 'dresses' in those early reports) with a burgundy coat and accessories. I'm intrigued by the reporter's knowledge of fabrics. Wedding reporting in local papers was a serious business and a necessary record. Black and white photos – or enhanced ones from photographic studios – were all that remained after the event. I have the pictures still, the bouquet trailing over the sweeping train and veil. Audrey stands demure, looking straight ahead with her mouth gently closed and smiling. What was she thinking? So much preparation had gone into the event and her parents were too ill to be there.

## Early married life

Audrey and Doug's new house at 13 Robertson Street was ready to move into straight after their honeymoon at Strathavon, a guesthouse on the Wyong River. Their comfortable red brick and tile house was built to last, typical of the unadorned style of the time. Each morning Doug rode his motorbike to the Steelworks, which he could see from his house. He was a young man in his first job, learning fast about all the vagaries of the steel business.

In the first year of marriage, Doug and Audrey became the primary carers for Gertrude and Alfred, who were both ill and bed-ridden. When I look at photos I wonder why my grandparents seem so much older than people their age today. With no penicillin, no labour-saving devices and few beauty products, life was more taxing then and it showed. With a house full of sick parents and pregnant, Audrey probably thought things couldn't get worse but she was wrong. Her first son was still-born, the cord wrapped tightly around his neck, though he was otherwise a perfectly formed, full-term child. At this time in Port Kembla there was no specialised obstetrical service, just a small private hospital, the midwife, and, if you were lucky, a GP with some experience in dealing with emergencies.

The hard times weren't over. Audrey's mother died in 1940, a year after the marriage. A few months later her father died. In 1941 their second son, David was born and shortly afterwards they discovered he was deaf. My father had been infected with German measles at work and passed it on to Audrey. At that time no one knew that German measles caused deafness. It wasn't until the 1941 Australian epidemic, when over 200 children, including David, were born deaf, that an Australian doctor, Norman Gregg, established a connection between the virus and deafness. My father never forgave himself.

I enter the picture in 1943 at a private hospital in Port Kembla. Dr Luscombe, a friend of our family's, and Nurse Watts helped me into the world. During the pregnancy my mother was encouraged to eat up and the result was black-haired, overweight me. After my mother's previous maternity experiences everyone was ensuring that I not only survived but was extremely healthy. Audrey said she couldn't stop smiling when she first saw me.

Audrey and Pam

In spite of setbacks, my parents enjoyed Port Kembla life. They played tennis and golf. Audrey was an organist at St Stephen's Church and Doug was involved with the Scouts. They had a wide social circle which lasted through the forties and fifties. Many of the young men who came to Port Kembla to work married Audrey's friends. I have pictures of them during their courting days, playing tennis, golf, swimming and on picnics together. Jean Pratt, her childhood friend, married Gus Parrish, Bertha Lee married Jack Thompson. Once married, they met in each other's houses, sharing food and sang their favourite songs round each other's pianos. The industries were the glue that bound them all together.

13

# Steelmaking and my father

With the takeover of AIS by BHP, Port Kembla prospered. There's nothing like a monopoly to aid a company's fortunes. BHP now controlled all iron and steelmaking in Australia and went on to tie up the whole steelmaking business, buying coal mines and expanding its shipping interests. It had gained government support for a large integrated industrial system. With all this investment came huge development. By 1936, BHP Port Kembla employed 3,700 workers, and one of them was my father.[1]

He worked there for 40 years and became superintendent of the coke ovens. He lived and breathed the process. Every morning and evening a foreman rang to report on the state of the ovens. I'd listen, absorbing the jargon, alert for problems, knowing it was a dangerous process and that men had died on his watch. My father had a stutter and unfortunately the letters he struggled with were 'D' and 'N', the first letters of his name. I'd sit close, mouthing his name, Doug Nock, willing the words to come.

His idea of a Sunday outing was to pack us into our Morris Oxford and go searching for coal mines in the hills around Wollongong. We'd groan, but nothing stopped him. He'd park and be out of the car and off, reappearing happily later to tell us about some abandoned mine he'd found. There were several opportunities for him to progress up the employment ladder, but they involved moving to Whyalla and other distant places. He stayed put because of David's need for special deaf education – it was relatively easy to get him to school in Sydney from Port Kembla, not so easy from places like Whyalla. Doug invested all his energy into steelmaking.

Highlights of his working life were several trips to Germany, where he wined and dined with steel magnates and was flown around in their planes to see various steelmaking operations. The same magnates continued to send him wines from the Moselle region every Christmas. When he retired he was invited to join the Pig Iron Club in Wollongong, a special group of men like him who had the same passion. For a retirement present the men from the coke ovens built him a steel garden composter with a revolving drum. It now lives in my country garden. My father's obsession with heavy industry was always a mystery to me. But occasionally at weekends he drove to check some part of the process and I would go with him and watch from a distance as slices of red-hot, incandescent coke tumbled out of the ovens like huge slices of volcanic toast. I've never forgotten them. It must be in my blood because I admit now I would be sad if the steel industry disappeared from Port Kembla.

14

# 1940s: Port Kembla and war

The war coincided with the first six years of my parents' marriage and affected them in different ways. BHP was prospering because of the increased demand for steel and my father was busy. Although he had a baby son, he wanted to enlist but was told to remain at work because his job was part of an essential industry. He assuaged some of his patriotic feeling by acting as the local air raid warden for the Volunteer Defence Corps (VDC). As the air raid siren was right outside his gate there was no chance he'd miss calls. When there was increased Japanese ship activity in the seas surrounding Port Kembla in 1941 and an attack seemed likely, he sent my mother and baby brother to stay with my paternal grandmother in Adelaide for two months. This was common practice: I know many mothers and children who moved away from the town, some to the Southern Highlands, during the war. My mother had an ambivalent relationship with my grandmother Elsie, and I wonder if that ambivalence began at this time. Elsie came from a long line of schoolteachers who thought there was a right way of doing everything.

Even though I wasn't born until 1943, I believe I remember the sound of the siren and sheltering under the heavy kitchen table belonging to our neighbour, Mrs Baxter. My cousin Gordon, four years older, definitely recalls the sound of the siren and how scared he felt, even though he lived a street away. Anne Mitchell, daughter of Audrey's friend Jean Pratt and born in 1939, remembers her heavily pregnant mother directing herself and her twin sister, Margaret to go down to the hill to their uncle's air raid shelter and remain there until late at night while her father and uncle listened to radio broadcasts upstairs. She also recollects soldiers appearing out of nowhere, popping their heads over the fence and saying, 'Hello girls' while she was playing in the garden with her sister.

Port Kembla was at peak preparedness. One hundred and twenty troops were stationed at the Breakwater Battery at the harbour entrance. Two ex-Naval guns capable of firing shells a distance of 16 kilometres stood ready. And there was action: between 1940 and 1944, 22 Allied ships struck Japanese mines or were torpedoed off the coast with 244 lives lost. At night Japanese U-boats signalled to each other with flares and twice Japanese spotter planes were sighted looking for targets. There are remnants of this war in the large concrete triangles which rest on the green grass above the entrance to Port Kembla Harbour. It's hard to imagine now, but these were tank traps, once positioned close to the shore to prevent Japanese tanks landing and invading from ships lurking nearby. These pyramidal fortifications of reinforced concrete are also known as Dragon's Teeth and were used for the first time during the

Second World War, mainly in Europe. By putting the structures in irregular rows the aim was to slow down the vehicles so that anti-tank guns could dispose of them easily.

Port Kembla had something very special to offer the war effort. Evelyn Owen, a 24-year-old Wollongong man who loved playing around with guns, invented a submachine gun as a teenager. He submitted his design to the Army but it was rejected. He was called up by the AIF shortly afterwards and, having to dispose of the gun somewhere, he dumped it in a sugar bag in the garage of one of his father's rental properties. If it wasn't for Vincent Wardell, that might have been the end of the story. Wardell was acting manager of Lysaghts at Port Kembla and rented the property where the gun had been left. He found it, recognised the clever design and its potential, and rang Essington Lewis, Minister of Munitions. A surprised Evelyn (Evo) was abruptly dismissed from the AIF and brought back home to help develop the gun for production alongside Vincent and his brother Gerard, who was the Chief Engineer at Lysaghts.[1]

That wasn't the end of it, both Vincent's diplomatic skills and Gerard's technical skills were needed to shepherd the gun through production and persuade the reluctant Army to buy it. It took a phone call from Vincent to John Curtin, the prime minister, before the initial order was reinstated. During the war Lysaghts produced 45,479 Owen guns, as they became known, creating a major boost to local employment. The Australian Army used Evelyn's gun from 1943 to the mid-1960s. It was the only entirely Australian designed submachine gun of the

Second World War. The Americans also used it. Soldiers liked it because it was impossible to jam and named it the 'Diggers Darling'.[2]

Wollongong and Port Kembla sent many men to fight and women to nurse in the Second World War. Unlike the earlier war, it was not such a remote experience for those left behind. With better communications and moving pictures, no one was in any doubt about the horrors. My mother's friend Pat Darling, a nurse, brought us the news first-hand. She entered our lives when she married our neighbour Colin Darling in 1949. Pat's accounts helped me to understand about war, affecting someone I knew.

After the Japanese bombed Singapore in December 1941, Pat worked at Johor Bahru, where she tended those wounded in the air attacks. In January, she served in a makeshift hospital in Singapore, set up on a tennis court under a large marquee.

As Japanese troops approached, she was evacuated on 12 February 1942, with 64 other nurses on the heavily laden *Vyner Brooke.* The ship, carrying 330 men, women and children, headed south for Banka Strait as Japanese planes bombed Singapore. On 14 February, enemy planes strafed the *Vyner Brooke*, holed some lifeboats and dropped bombs on the guns and down the funnel. Pat helped load wounded people into two lifeboats then jumped into the oily sea before the ship disappeared. She clung to a floating spa among the wreckage and dead bodies until she was dragged onto a raft which she helped pull ashore as the Japanese were invading Sumatra.

Pat described her efforts to survive in an unemotional way: the hours in the sea clinging onto wreckage, withstanding the cruelty of the Japanese in the camp on Sumatra, the terrible hunger and illnesses, prisoners becoming so thin they fell into latrines and had to be pulled out. She was only 33 kilograms at the end of the war, when 'a person's eyes were like two burnt holes in a blanket' as she says in her 2001 memoir.[3] Her obituary in the *Sydney Morning Herald* in 2007 noted her resilience.[4]

How to acknowledge horrific war experiences like Pat's? Port Kembla did its best, beginning in 1923 with a granite plinth outside the RSL on the corner of Military and Darcy Roads. A plaque was attached naming the First World War dead, and the premier of New South Wales, the Hon. CW Oakes, laid a stone in commemoration. A captured German field gun, previously drawn by six horses, was placed nearby. The town now had its yearly gathering point.

And yet nothing lasts forever. In 2017 the RSL is up for sale and with it the land on which the memorial stands. However, Peter Poulton, sub-branch president, assured *Illawarra Mercury* readers that, 'My concerns were about the memorial but fortunately the contract for the sale keeps the memorial sacrosanct. Right-of-way will ensure residents of Port Kembla will have a permanent home for their memorial and a place for ceremonies on Anzac Day.'[5]

15

# Movers and shakers

Wars came and went while Port Kembla moved on with its affairs. The town attracted many talented people, but most early movers and shakers left little written down and have largely disappeared from the records. People are strangely absent from histories of Port Kembla. Previous writers have concentrated on trends, overviews of public events and tensions between capital and labour. In these accounts it's hard to imagine what it was like in early Port Kembla, where lives and events are reduced to patterns. The reality is more likely to have been messy and spontaneous – people making it up as they went along.

Trawling through newspapers of the early 1900s one name is mentioned more than most – HR Lee. He was a start-up, one-man-band kind of man. You name it, he began it: my family knew him well. I asked his granddaughter, Barbara Gassman (née White) what she thought motivated him. She said he was known in the family as an entrepreneur. 'Everywhere he went he started up things, in Captains Flat and Queanbeyan and later in Port Kembla.'

He packed a lot into a life shortened by an appendix operation that went wrong – he died at the age of 56. In 1922 he formed the Port Kembla Boy Scouts and in 1923 began the South Coast District Organisation of Scouts. He started the surf club, the Masonic lodge and the cricket club and during the First World War was recruiting officer and later repatriation officer for Port Kembla. He was largely responsible for the building of the Moss Vale train line. He was an alderman on the Central Illawarra Council for 14 years and secretary of the Port Kembla Progress Association. He supported the Lake Illawarra Entrance Bridge League, the Port Kembla Bowling Club and the Parents and Citizens Association. He worked as chief accountant at ER&S and later took up industrial law in 1918. He became the industrial officer for the three Port Kembla industries. In 1927 he was appointed secretary to the New South Wales branch of the Australian Mines and Metals Association and was regarded as one of Australia's best authorities on industrial matters. He met and married Alice Antill in Queanbeyan, New South Wales, and they had seven children. In his free time he went fishing, shooting and was a leading rugby league player. When he was younger and working in the copper industry in Captains Flat he showed similar energy for developing community organisations. HR Lee created many of the things in Port Kembla that were central to my life, and he was instrumental in establishing my favourite place, the Whiteway, our entertainment hub. His daughter Stella White sums up the nature of the man:

'In the early days of Port Kembla, where my parents went to live, my father became a legend. The nearest doctor was in Wollongong, four miles away and the other side of Tom Thumb Lagoon, over which there was no bridge for some years, and he attended to all first-aid cases in the township. People with all sorts of legal problems came to him for advice, and he was on every committee for the advancement and well-being of the people of the district.'

The White family was another group of movers and shakers and were connected to HR through marriage. (Leonard and Earnest White married Lee's daughters.) The first to be associated with Port Kembla was Edmond, their uncle. He was born in 1875 and grew up in Rockhampton and began working at Mount Morgan Gold Mining Company. In 1907, now married to Esther Hanley and with a small son, Rupert, he moved to New South Wales and started work at ER&S, first as superintendent of construction. He became manager in 1918 and general manager in 1926. Typical of men like him, he was active in local affairs as an advocate of the Moss Vale to Port Kembla railway, a foundation member of the Port Kembla golf club, president of the Chamber of Commerce and president of the Boy Scouts Association. His nephews Leonard and Earnest were also part of the business and social life of the town. Sets of brothers played an important part in Port Kembla's early history – Charles and Syd Hoskins (Steelworks) and Vincent and Gerard Wardell (Lysaghts) also gave much to the town.

***

Without services, towns fall back on the locals' skill sets, and in the early days of Port Kembla people were adept at starting up and running whatever they needed. Was it the collection of industries and entrepreneurial types that provided much of this get-up-and-go? Or was this a general trend in Australia at the time? Whatever it was, the coming together of Charles Jackson and the scouting movement was another success story for Port Kembla. In 1958 his services to Illawarra Scouting were recognised when his name appeared on the Queen's birthday honours list. He was indefatigable. Reading the *Illawarra Mercury* from the 1930s onwards his name appears in connection with anything related to scouting.

The account of the Corroboree Camp held in Port Kembla gives me some idea of his organising prowess. On Friday, 27 December 1930, by the shores of Lake Illawarra, scouts from all over the state, as well as some from South Australia and Queensland, pitched their tents in a semi-circle surrounding camp headquarters. Most of them had come by special train from Sydney. Some scouts from outback New South Wales hadn't seen a train before. They were divided into five tribes: Illawarra, Barrengary, Corrandeel, Wattamolla and Camberwarra. The scouts enjoyed gatherings round camp fires and prepared for the Monday march past before His Excellency the Governor General and Chief Scout of Australia, Sir Isaac Isaacs. (The first Australian to be appointed Governor General.) It rained on the day, but after a short delay the march-past and rally proceeded with the Port Kembla band playing. All was captured by Movietone

News. That wasn't the end of it, as the *Sunday Times* reported:

> On Tuesday morning the camp was astir early. Scouts left Port Kembla for various stations between Berry and Nowra which they used for jumping-off places for the hike. Scouts in their various tribes set out for the station. Just after leaving camp a heavy storm was experienced; some of the scouts were wet through and it was found necessary to send a small party back to camp. His Excellency was there to bid each tribe 'Good luck and a good hike' and as the Tribes passed, each in turn gave three cheers for their Chief. The Vice-Regal party left camp at 8 a.m. for Sydney. His Excellency expressed his thanks for what he termed 'a ripping time'.[1]

In September 2015 I visited Charles Jackson's son Brian at Farmborough Heights near Wollongong and asked him what had inspired his father. Brian said it all started when his friend Roy Woodhouse, a Sydney newspaper editor, gave him a copy of *Scouting for Boys*. Charles believed this was what Australian boys needed and together they decided to start up a troop at Waverley in Sydney, which was the first one in Australia.

Charles was born in 1898 and lived with his parents above a bank at 99 Pitt Street, Sydney. He came to Port Kembla in 1923 and stayed until the 1980s, when he left because of ill health. He was involved in everything: scouts, surf lifesaving, swimming clubs in both Wollongong and Port Kembla, the Five Islands Masonic Lodge, the golf club and the RSL. He was a superior sports person and swam for Australia during the First World War Olympics. Charles's secret weapon in all his endeavours was the scouts. When he needed workers for activities he called them up – or their parents. The surf lifesaving club started with scouts as volunteer life guards. Brian said the appeal of scouting for Charles was the discipline. He remembers as a child not being allowed out of the house unless his clothes were tidy, and his father was always dressed in a suit and tie.

'If he saw someone badly dressed he'd give them directions on how to get it right. For him a tidy person had a tidy mind.' His wife spent hours washing and ironing to maintain these standards. But in spite of this almost obsessive preoccupation, Brian remembers him as a gentle man with a sense of humour who was willing to help anyone.

He was called 'Chief' by everyone and Brian explained why. Charles began the Austinmer Scout Club in 1923 while living as a bachelor in Tersco Lane, Port Kembla. Austinmer to Port Kembla was a long slow trip. He walked five miles (eight kilometres) to the station, caught the train to Austinmer and walked another five miles to the scout hall. Sir Vincent Fairfax, a supporter of the scouts, wanted to help and bought him an Indian Chief motorcycle. This allowed Charles to do the whole trip in one speedy go. He worked for General Agency as a salesman of electrical appliances and travelled up and down the coast selling their latest goods. This job was a neat fit for him, as he managed to be in each town when scout meetings were scheduled. Brian said scouts was never far from his father's mind.

Charles Jackson, along with Charles and Syd Hoskins, wanted a scout camp for New South Wales to stage big events and in 1940 they opened one at Mount Keira on land belonging to Australian Iron and Steel. The company paid for much of its upkeep. I often visited this beautiful rainforest site as it was near where my parents lived after they moved from Port Kembla. A road winds down through lush ferns and huge trees to a green lawn. On 7 November 2015, the scouts' seventy-fifth anniversary was celebrated there with the scouts camped in the clearing. Charles's portrait still hangs in one of the buildings. The land has since been taken over by National Parks and Wildlife and the scouts are expected to pay their way. To help with this, weddings are held on the site most weekends.

Charles Jackson, typical of other Port Kembla polymaths, was not content with one or two areas of endeavour. There was nothing he wouldn't try – including opening a funeral parlour in the 1960s. Brian explained how this came about. One day he was talking to his friend Bill Rankin on his back verandah and noted that with 28 deaths a day, one funeral parlour in the town wasn't enough. Bill said he could run it. Charles asked if he knew anything about the business. Bill said not much but he was willing to learn. Which is what he did after resigning as employment officer for Metal Manufactures. The business was called the Bill Rankin Funeral Parlour. This improvised approach was the usual way of doing business in Port Kembla at this time.

16

# A 1950s snapshot

**Photo of Wentworth Street taken by Frank Hurley in the 1950s**
The National Library, PIC:FH/7327 LOC. COLDSTORE. PICHURL. 227/13

It's challenging capturing the lively buzz of how it was. Reasons for the town's prosperity were diverse. Although not achieving the autonomy it wanted when the Central Illawarra Council amalgamated with the local councils of Bulli, Northern Illawarra and Wollongong to form the Greater City of Wollongong in 1947, success came to the Port in other guises.[1]

The influx of migrants brought vibrant energy. Thousands of mostly displaced people came from Europe searching for work and settled in and around the town. During the 1950s the Steelworks expanded, building the No. 1 Coke Battery, a hot strip mill and a tinplate production plant. Two blast furnaces were also commissioned: No. 3 in 1952 and the Open Hearth – the largest blast furnace at that time in Australia – was opened by Essington Lewis, Australia's leading industrialist, in 1956.[2] Making steel became more efficient after the building of the inner harbour in 1960. Four million cubic metres of mud were dredged and 340,000 cubic metres of rock blasted before it was finally done and a traffic of raw and finished products began shipping in and out. With production accelerating, migrants were absorbed into all sections of the vast business. By 1963 the workforce of 15,000 was turning out 3 million tonnes of steel annually. In 1950, the *Sydney Morning Herald* reported:

> By the end of the next year the rapidly growing South Coast industrial centre will have a steel-producing capacity 25 per cent greater than Newcastle, which for 35 years had been the unchallenged home of the Australian steel industry.[3]

Many of these workers and their families came to Wentworth Street, Port Kembla, for their shopping. Happy store owners geared up for extra business and we all benefited from the increased variety of goods. The street was packed with VJ Holdens, men wore hats and women dressed up in waisted, full-skirted dresses and hats. A Greek family ran the milk bar on the corner of Hall and Wentworth Streets and made their own sweet treats. My favourites were strawberry malted milkshakes and chocolate-coated Turkish delight. On summer evenings my family and others strolled up and down the steep street, window shopping. We admired diamond rings and glassware on display in the window of Chiragakis jewellery store. We gathered to watch the test patterns outside the shop selling new televisions. We checked out the clothes available at Claussens store, which had been there since 1938 suppling the town's clothing needs, including school uniforms. I ignored the stairs leading up to the rooms of Mr Esdale, the dentist. With no fluoride in the water and sweets and cakes readily available, my teeth were terrible. The dentist did his best, but with minimal anaesthetics and constant visits I'm not a keen visitor to the dentist.

The street had everything: a cake shop, an electrical store, a pharmacy, Commonwealth and National banks, a fruit shop and Mr Kemp the grocer. Fairleys, an important fixture in my grandmother's time, was still a thriving haberdashery. The library, which opened in 1948 in the former Presbyterian Church, was central to our lives. Several tennis courts in the main street were available for hire. The well-liked Dr Luscombe had a surgery nearby. Churches were there: Methodist and Catholic in parallel streets and the Anglican was up the top near the public school. The Scout Hall in Hall Street was busy with cubs, scouts, ballet and tap. My mother and I often walked past the hall on our way up the long hill leading home to Robertson Street and I'd ask, 'Why can't I learn tap-dancing?'

'It's not lady-like.'

The metallic sound of tap shoes still gives me a buzz.

Not that new residents felt much of a buzz. Many had come from cosmopolitan places offering a range of cultural activities, homes to great composers like Chopin. In comparison Port Kembla was a ghost town after dark. But the Poles got cracking, they wanted to recreate their culture in their new neighbourhood. One of their priests, Father Arciszewski, began a Polish school in the local Catholic Church hall in 1955. In 1956, the Independent Polish Association was established in the same hall. They replicated their world, ate their favourite food (sauerkraut and borscht), danced their traditional dances, dressed in their national costume and spoke their native language.

## 17

# Putting myself in the picture

I have never forgotten the smell of rotten egg gas. As children we took for granted the pervading smog and the stench of lead and sulphur dioxide fumes and the fine dust over everything. It wasn't until the westerly blew the gunk out to sea that we came to life. My father never admitted the negative side of his work and believed sulphur fumes helped grow the best peaches, insisting they killed bugs. Gillie Evans, who lived in Private Lane, remembers walking to school and hating the days the winds sent the toxic vapours her way. She wonders how we're still alive. And yet the upside of 1950s Port Kembla was its energetic vibrancy.

My life revolved around home, school and church, but the fun part was the cinema. I was lucky as there were two ladies living in our street who also loved the movies. Every Saturday afternoon Mrs Morton and Mrs Baxter walked down the hill to the Whiteway on Wentworth Street where two or sometimes three films would be screened, and we children tagged along. Did we invite ourselves or did these large-hearted ladies allow us to join them to give our parents a rest? Mrs Morton was a small, storybook character and always carried a commodious bag. Mrs Baxter was taller, more practical and kept us in check. They were benign beings, their cake-plump bodies swathed in layers of browny-grey fabric with squashy hats on their heads and seemingly just there for us. I have no memory of them having husbands but both had grown-up children living at home.

We wore our best clothes, we girls in our birthday dresses with ribbons in our hair, and were always on time for the first film starting at 2.00 p.m. In the cavernous space of the cinema the ladies sat up the back and we sat close enough for their lolly drip feed. Westerns, musicals, cartoons – the lot, we rollicked through, loving the plots and not really affected until *Bambi*. I can still summon up emotion at the memory of Bambi's mother being killed – it was the worst thing I could imagine, my mother dying.

## School

School was not my favourite place. In 1950 a kindergarten boy from my street wet his pants, gasping sobs of relief when his mother came to rescue him in the afternoon – I was relieved it wasn't me. We were expected to become independent quickly and by the end of First Class I was walking home with my friends. No Finnish forest schools for us, just bad-tempered teachers and a smoggy, rough and tumble playground. By Fifth Class I was a school refuser. Every morning my mother said, 'Off you go, it will be all right when you get there.' What would she know? There was Mrs Cross, who lived up to her name and threw inkwells when annoyed. Mean-eyed Mrs Moe, infuriated by my left-handed sewing, ruined me for life when she barked, 'Any fool can do it,' throwing down my chain stitch sampler in disgust. I was often in trouble for no apparent reason and spent time with my friend Sue outside the door of the headmistress, Miss Wade, waiting for her cane-rap over the knuckles. Ann Mitchell has similar memories:

> Mrs P was a terrible lady. We were in class after lunch and Mrs P asked who had left their cardigan in the playground. I had, but didn't own up. She said if no one admitted it was their cardigan she'd hit everyone with the wooden end of her feather duster. I stood up and said it was mine. She ordered me to come and stand near her desk and hit me twice over the back of the hand. On her third attempt I pulled away my hand and the duster hit her beloved desk. She was livid.

In the classroom four rows of wooden desks were lined up facing the front. Each week there were tests that decided where you sat. Everyone was ranked according to how well they did in the tests. I was happy to cling, with two Sues and a girl called Robyn, to one of the top four places at the back of the right-hand row. We had girls-only classes from Third Class, but once we were out in the playground there were boys. I dreaded Friday afternoon maypole dancing and can still feel the warty hands of my boy partner.

I developed an aversion to school, knowing there was something better. Every morning I set off with Sue, a student at St Patrick's, the Catholic school, a neat and tidy place in a suburban street that was on my way. I would walk on, wanting to stay in her well-disciplined playground supervised by smiling nuns. Port Kembla Public, abutting busy, smelly, noisy industry, was a war zone by comparison. Sue later became a nun.

## In the neighbourhood

In the 1950s we called each other's parents 'Mr' and 'Mrs' and didn't interrupt adult conversations, but in many ways we were free. During the holidays and after school we ranged around the area and our parents had little idea where we were. There was one rule: be home by 6 p.m. We found fun where we could; it might be a game of fiddlesticks on the bedroom carpet of one of two friends called Sue. Her house was immaculate and I shape-shifted accordingly: polite, yes-thank-you, no-thank-you, tailoring my interests to suit quieter games like drawing and reading. We were starved for books and got hooked on series, swapping, borrowing and begging for birthdays. I've long forgotten the name of the author of *Anne of Green Gables*, but Anne's world I still remember. My mother's cousin, Irma, worked for Gordon and Gotch book distributors in Melbourne and brought me girls annuals on her frequent visits. I got the better end of the deal as she'd take to her bed for weeks and my mother had to look after her.

Out on the street there was always something happening: hopscotch, skipping with huge thick ropes, cricket, rounders and making things. Fresh from the garage workshop, made from leftover kindling, we raced our billy carts down the hill towards Keira Street. On windy days we flew hand-made kites in the high paddock behind our house. We built stilts with tin cans and rope, loving our giant selves. We lived outside as did our mothers. Audrey chatted over the fence to Mrs Baxter as she hung out the washing or checked her rows of beans and peas growing on the trellis.

On overcast days there were indoor games: cards, dominoes, writing and drawing in each other's autograph books. I still remember one of my favourite inscriptions, written by my mother: '*Lost in an impenetrable forest and surrounded by wolves.*' Boys played and swapped marbles and girls, locked out, retreated into growing magic gardens and make-believe. If it rained and we wanted something messy there were mud pies. Although I wasn't a doll person, I was shocked years later when Rosemary, my one and only doll, was broken. With its large china face and staring eyes, it seemed real.

The ABC's *The Argonauts Club* on the radio was an essential part of my world and when I heard the opening song calling old Mother Hubbard and Tom the Piper's son I would race to the room where our console radio was kept. Clubs were a central part of life. What was different about the Argonauts was the emphasis on writing. We sent in work, got feedback, and if we were lucky it was read out. The show developed a lifelong love of myth, history and literature in its listeners. We were given a boat and oar number and journeyed to find the Golden Fleece. I loved saying the pledge each night, '*Before the sun and the night and the blue sea, I vow to stand faithfully by all that is brave and beautiful.*'

My mother enjoyed words and often read to me, books like Charles Kingsley's *The Water Babies* with characters such as Mrs-Do-As-You-Would Be-Done-By. Over several sessions of the Argonauts I heard Ruth Park's *The Wideawake Bunyip*, which changed its name to *The Muddle-Headed Wombat* in 1951 when the actor who read the part of Joe, Albert Collins, died.

Into my teenage years I played dress-ups with a group of friends. My mother kept a suitcase filled with old dresses, hats and fur stoles. In our adopted personae we strutted up and down Robertson Street acting out another life for an hour or two. I have a faded photo of us draped over an old truck belonging to a neighbour, looking oddly raunchy with our garish lipstick and sophisticated clothes. Or I would race down the hill, lured by a deluxe gramophone with speakers in a wooden cabinet that belonged to the family of my friend Gillian Pratt. We loved Bill Haley and the Comets' 'Rock Around the Clock' and shouted and shimmied, high on the beat, little knowing we were being primed for the 1960s. Hanging about in each other's houses for hours, soaking up other people's lives was a fallback activity. I considered my cousin Diana's house glamorous with its plush red carpet and formal dining room. I also liked visiting my other friend Sue's house because her family was different from mine and unexpected things happened. One day Sue's father cut off a chicken's head in preparation for cooking and the body ran around headless. Her parents smoked cigarettes and drank – edgy by my parents' standards.

Until the late 1950s, with no television, there was a lot of time to fill. Building a tree-house took days. We collected wood, built a ladder, hammered the whole thing together, arranged furniture, established a look-out and decided what to do. Secret societies with complicated rules and practices were popular. After school and during holidays we spent hours in the tree-house. We'd pull up the ladder and inhabit our own universe. It was a shock at night to return to our parents' world and their rules.

'Keep your elbows off the table.'

'Dessert only if you eat your vegetables.'

Once I sat in front of a plate of spinach, refusing to eat it and refusing to leave the table. My mother, worn out by my endurance, caved in and gave me stewed fruit and ice cream made with Carnation milk. Another evening, when I about ten, I was late home and didn't arrive until after dark; it was the only time my father ever hit me: disciplinary words first, then a small whack with his belt. I was sent to bed without dinner while my mother hovered in the background, not knowing what to do.

What we loved more than anything were firecrackers and bonfire nights. Bonfire Night had begun as a way to commemorate Queen Victoria (the date, 24 May, was her birthday), however the significance of the date was lost on us. As soon as the weather cooled, the rituals of shopping for supplies and collecting wood began. We'd save for weeks and once we had enough money, we'd buy a few crackers: double bungers, Catherine wheels, rockets, roman candles, jumping jacks and sparklers which were available at corner shops and newsagencies. We'd inspect our stash regularly – counting, skiting. The rest of the lead-up time was spent watching (or occasionally helping) the older boys building the bonfire on a vacant block, its wigwam shape growing higher and higher. It was the most important ritual we could imagine.

On the night itself, desperate not to miss the lighting of the bonfire, we ran down the hill after our 6 p.m. dinner to be there for the first whoosh of flame and the first rockets. Not that I let mine off there. I lit my hoarded treasure one at a time, outside our house. My father helped with the nailing of Catherine wheels to posts and the launching of rockets. My brother David, who had a taste for adventurous activities, loved the jumping jacks and bungers which fizzed and banged in unpredictable ways. Later, with the smell of saltpetre, sulphur and charcoal in the air, we drifted off to sleep – every nascent pyromaniac bone in our bodies satisfied.

Birthday parties were another important ritual. We counted down the days, knowing what to expect, but loving them all the same. I have photos of us in our party clothes and wearing hats we'd made, lined up behind the cake. We were lucky as Mrs Baxter, our next-door neighbour, was good at fancy baking. The cake she made for my brother David was a facsimile of a train engine with wheels and funnels and covered in sweets. My mother's efforts were lopsided and overly pinked with cochineal, although she cooked other food perfectly.

**David and friends at his birthday. He is three from the left and I am kneeling beside him.**

Parties were held at each other's houses and the games were much the same: pass the parcel, three-legged and egg-and-spoon races. If sacks were available there was a sack race. We organised our own games, dragging heavy chairs into place for musical chairs. For every event someone won a prize. We ate cocktail frankfurters, chocolate crackles, jelly set in orange halves, fairy bread, meringues and lemonade. We liked gardens with trees for climbing and houses with hidden places. We checked out new birthday toys and books before going home with a bag of lollies. One friend, Lindley, had the best parties, first in her house in Reservoir Street where my grandparents had once lived and then in a more luxurious company house.

Each year before my September birthday my mother bought me a special dress which I later wore to Sunday School and parties. I insisted on wearing it immediately, even if the weather was cold. I still remember the go-anywhere feeling of the one I received when I turned 13 – it was made out of blue gingham with three tiers of flounces, a scooped frilled neck and full skirt under which I wore a rope petticoat.

My mother, a great fan of Christmas, always made it special. I'd wake up, feel for a full pillowcase at the end of the bed and, finding it there, go back to sleep. Presents were simple: smelly soap, something to read, books of tricks, and magic gardens which came to life in water. One year was different. I was ten and when I woke up there was a bike leaning against my bed. It wasn't new but I didn't care. My father had painted it and made it roadworthy. It was my escape vehicle, and took me anywhere I wanted. One time, without telling our parents, I rode to Shellharbour with my friend Sue. With the wind in my face, pedalling as fast as I could and a friend by my side, doing something risky – it was perhaps the freest I've ever felt.

## Animals

In the 1950s, bitsers were the best we could do – there were no fancy pedigrees or vaccinations from vets for our dogs. We handled our own emergencies – I remember my ashen father drowning a clutch of kittens in a bucket in the back garden. My brother had a series of kelpies that started as appealing puppies and morphed into huge, out-of-control beasts. They placed their paws on our shoulders and licked us with sloppy affection. My mother shooed them away when guests arrived.

One of our dogs, Sox, couldn't believe its luck after we moved to Mount Keira. It ranged around the mountain, trying out dimly remembered ancestral hunting skills on the neighbours' unsuspecting sheep. Farmers were livid.

There was always a dog around when I was a child and everyone knew Peter Darling's kelpie, Brownie. It was Peter's shadow, going to school with him even though it wasn't allowed. Peter remembers Brownie following him all the way down Keira Street, past the Presbyterian Church, then lurking behind bushes and disappearing under the school's portable classroom so it wouldn't be spotted. There it mostly stayed until the afternoon walk home. However, when the ER&S whistle blew, alerting volunteer fire-fighters that they were needed at the fire station in nearby Military Road, Brownie howled a terrible howl, the siren stirring up some deep emotion. This gave away its hiding place and an exasperated headmaster, Mr Townsend, regularly called Peter in, saying, 'Is that Brownie again? Get rid of him!'

Packs of stray dogs roamed around Port Kembla and my cousin Diana and I brought some home. My mother put up with this until the red setter day. Most strays were mangy-coated, but not this one. Sleek and charismatic, he loped along, happy to guzzle water from the tap and settle on our back landing. I was proud that he had chosen me, and imagined days prowling the town together. As night fell, I checked he was still there. When he grew restless, not wanting to lose him I let him into the kitchen. He bounded to the stove and with one sweep of his beautiful tawny head gulped the saucepan of cooling mince before I could do a thing.

'Mum, something terrible's happened!'

My mother wasn't happy as we'd have nothing to eat that night, but couldn't help laughing.

'We can't afford to keep him.'

Even I could see that – a dog who ate dinner for four as an appetiser was out of our price range. I put him back on the landing and the next morning he was gone.

When herds of wild horses visited the paddock behind our house we were happy. They came in summer when the grass was long. Boys tried to lasso and ride them. Were the horses the progeny of animals used to pull the sulkies of my grandparents?

When I was young, animals were also a central part of our entertainment life. We knew it was summer when circuses came to town and pitched their tents by Lake Illawarra. Some days I'd ride down with Sue to check out what was happening. We were warned away from the lions in their too-small cages. The atmosphere was edgy and not particularly welcoming – everyone was focused on creating the evening's event. Tents were raised by strong swarthy men; jugglers, acrobats and clowns practised their routines.

At night we sat with our parents under the big top on tiered planks. The whole place smelt of sawdust, animal urine and sweat. No wonder the circus people were unfriendly, the whole operation ran close to disaster. Girls stood on galloping horses with a ringmaster cracking his whip, lions were out of their cages but, still unhappy, baulked before jumping through hoops of fire. High-wire gymnasts balanced, sometimes without a safety net. The miniature fox terriers dressed in jackets and ties that did balancing tricks on seesaws were my favourites. After it was over and everything had been loaded onto huge trucks during the night and the lake paddock left empty, we felt abandoned.

I wondered how hard it would be to stage a circus. I already knew a few tricks as my mother had bought me a book on magic. Deep in never-ending summer holidays I invited my friends to magic shows and they'd sit round our table while I ran through my repertoire: lots of items disappearing and reappearing and tricks with water glasses. Because my mother always backed up with something good to eat, I was never short of an audience. One time I directed my friends to teach their pet a trick and arranged a date for us to put on a circus on the large grassy space beside our house. On the day there was a reasonable turnout: dogs mostly, happy to be part of the game. Our family was between kelpies and all I had was Toby, our grey tabby. I dressed it in my old baby clothes, including a matching bonnet knitted by my mother using complicated, lacy stitches. I put Toby in my old pram and we all walked in a large wavering circle, our mothers watching. Toby was unhappy from the beginning, hissing, yowling and shooting glances of hatred at me. Before I could do a thing, it leapt out, scrambled up the back fence, the bonnet still hanging by its ribbons around its neck. On the top of the fence it paused for a moment, looking like some nightmare baby an anxious pregnant mother might dream up, before disappearing into the long grass of the back paddock.

## Church

Church was a central part of my childhood. My parents were married at St Stephen's, Port Kembla. My mother played the organ, belonged to the church guild, did the flowers, sat on committees and entertained visiting clerics. My father, once he made the move from the Methodist Church down the road, also became an active participant. I went to Sunday School, sang '*Hear the pennies dropping …*' and later taught Sunday School and sang in the choir. Highlights were Easter, Harvest Festival, the spring flower show and Christmas. I was immersed in the seasonal life of the church, believing it all to be true and good.

My favourite event was the spring flower show, held in the hall behind the church. I enjoyed the preparations, helping my mother who was on the committee: setting up trestles, unpacking parcels of goods, the cups of tea and acres of sweet things. I loved it when the flowers arrived: huge dahlias carried in by growers, saucers of pansies without their stalks, and roses of every colour. I watched as exhibits were labelled and everyone checked out each other's entries. Dressed in our best we would arrive for the show, exhilarated by the noise and heady perfumes of the flowers. We admired the winners in each category, bought toffee apples, knitted toys and second-hand books. Sometimes we sang, standing on the stage looking down at our parents, who smiled approval while eating jam and scones.

Easter's see-sawing emotional journey sucked me in. As soon as the palm fronds were tied to the pews, a sense of foreboding set in. By Good Friday, with its sad hymns, I was sunk in melancholy and relieved when the bells of Easter Sunday rang out and we were back to normal. Harvest Festival, with the altar loaded with pumpkins and sheaves of corn from the farmers in the congregation and singing *'All things bright and beautiful'*, was much easier on the emotions.

At Christmas there were buckets of blue hydrangeas waiting in our laundry tub ready for the huge vases either side of the church altar. I remember the process: cut the stems, pop them straight into boiling water, count to twenty and then plunge them into cold water. My mother and her helpers would gather in the church and arrange the heavy-headed flowers.

In my early teens I joined the choir and there were the descant parts of hymns to learn and sections of '*The Messiah*'. The church was packed on the Sunday before Christmas for the lesson and carol service. Owen Dykes, the energetic minister, led the service with vestments billowing and his beautiful tenor voice rising above the singing of the congregation. It was my mother's most anxious day on the organ. Morning service on Christmas Day was a more relaxed affair. My mother, released from her duties, and my father at his most jovial, chatted to their friends before returning home. I was always in a hurry to get back to my new books before we filled ourselves with roast chicken, pickled pork and plum pudding – my grandmother Gertrude's recipe, of course.

Around about the time I was confirmed, on 27 October 1957, the evangelical students came to town. Was it Billy Graham's influence? Whatever it was I remember a constant stream of mission-intense young men. My parents fed them and I hung around. There were often events in the church hall and visits from dignitaries, including the Archbishop of Sydney, Dr Loane. At one event, when I was 14, he put his hand on my shoulder and asked, 'Are you saved?'

'I'm not sure,' I mumbled.

I won the Divinity Prize in Sixth Class. All through my childhood, my parents were deeply involved with the church and I went along. But questions were starting to form. One year in high school, before the hockey season, our headmistress, thinking it would toughen us up before the local competition, arranged a game with a collection of clerics. They were beyond ferocious, stopping at nothing to gain a point, whacking shins and breaking rules. We won, but I never felt quite the same. By the time I left school, the seasonally ritualistic life of the church that I'd accepted unquestioningly for so long was over for me.

## A different 1950s perspective

Growing up, my brother and I lived different lives. Until I spoke to him recently I believed his childhood an unhappy one. He was deaf and local schools were not equipped to teach children like him so he went away to Sydney for his education, coming home each Friday evening. I remember my parents' anxiety when he finished school and at other times when he seemed at risk: once accidentally shooting himself in the hand with a gun belonging to Peter Morton, one of our neighbours, and later the fallout from a joyride in a car.

I want to talk to him. When we were young we communicated easily using finger spelling, but now Auslan is the preferred way of signing and my skills aren't good enough. I ask David's son Robert, who worked for a time as an interpreter for the deaf, to help me. From the ensuing conversation I find out more than I've ever known.

Being sent away to the School for Deaf in Darlington seemed like banishment to me, but David didn't see it that way. He liked being among other deaf children and looked forward to the ease of sign language communication. Even though the cane was used at his school, the teachers were generally supportive. He enjoyed the lessons, especially history and woodwork, and when he was older he was responsible for the younger children, helping them in the boarding house and teaching them soccer and cricket. He was lucky, he went home at weekends; other children didn't. There were four or five who went up from Wollongong each Monday, so there was company on the train to Sydney and he looked forward to coming home on Fridays and being looked after by Audrey. I worried about Doug never learning to sign but David said he didn't mind, seeing him as a stern but kind parent.

He liked Port Kembla where he rode his bike to visit friends, went swimming and saw movies. As a child he loved building things and taking toy cars apart, though he admitted he couldn't always put them back together. He appreciated our double garage, one set aside as a workshop, where he built billy carts and later yachts, including a catamaran, which he sailed on Lake Illawarra. Drawings were sent by mail from a sailing company in Brookvale and David built the boats from scratch. On his hands he spelt out why he liked sailing: 'It was peaceful, relaxing out on the water, all together watching the other boats.'

Peter Darling, who lived opposite, remembers David as an adventurous person, always in the thick of things, hanging out with a group of boys from the street including him and Godfrey and Alan Mills. They found their own fun. Sometimes they fished for eels in the old quarry. As eels could eat through ordinary fishing lines they used thick hooked wire. Peter remembers David being particularly good at this. The gang was always making things. One day they shaped a canoe out of corrugated iron and put an abandoned toilet seat on top, sealing it together with tar begged from workers on the roads. They strapped it on to one of their bikes and cycled down to Coomaditchie Lagoon where they paddled around looking for wild duck eggs.

David remembered the kindness of our next-door neighbour, Mrs Baxter, who fed him cakes and paid him to mow her lawn. The older Baxter son, Jack, later employed him as an apprentice fitter and turner at Garnocks, an engineering works in Port Kembla, which is still carrying out repairs on ships in the nearby harbour. The five yachts David built in our garage more than prepared him for this kind of work. I asked how he managed the fitting and turning course at TAFE with no interpreters available. He said he found the maths and practical side easy and thought they probably made allowances in the written section because of his deafness. At Garnocks he worked on huge steel motors, accessing them from a moveable floor which was lowered or raised in order to reach the part needing attention. His school friend Trevor also worked at Garnocks, in the carpentry section. They often met for lunch and discussed what they were doing. David became a leading hand and worked at a variety of engineering works. He brushed off my suggestion that today with better teaching methods he would have been an engineer. He is not resentful about his deafness and has enjoyed his life.

18

# Beaches of the Port

I led my life against a backdrop of blast furnaces, chimneys and factories. Industrial smoke filled the air and my nose. However, alongside the man-made world was one of physical beauty. From our house on the hill I could see lagoon, lake and sea with one sweep of the eye. I took this duality for granted, but was dimly aware something was under threat. This awareness didn't stop me revelling in long, chilled-out beach days in my shirred bubble costume, zinc slathered on my nose, under an umbrella with other families nearby doing the same. Port Kembla beach stretches for 6.6 kilometres – the longest in the Illawarra, a perfect semicircle of sand and water with the hilly escarpment a blue haze in the distance. There is also a rock platform beside the beach where shellfish and other liminal creatures live in tidal pools. Somehow the land adjoining the beach has been protected from development and it looks much the same now as it always has. Since 1937 an Olympic swimming pool has encouraged swimmers to fine-tune their strokes and I remember being impressed when John and Ilsa Konrads gave a demonstration there in the 1950s.

On my childhood beach, life had a perpetual lazy afternoon, set-in-aspic feel. We walked about two kilometres from Robertson Street, through the sand dunes, skirting an Aboriginal camp made out of packing cases and sugar bags, a sad remnant of the proud people who once moved freely here.

We rushed to buy when the pie man called. I peered into pools around the rocks and watched crabs and other animals going about their business. I was calmed by the swish of water at my feet. Once a baby penguin floated by on choppy waves. I was impressed when cousin John steered his surf board, long by today's standards, towards the shore. I was not keen on swimming lessons in the nearby pool. The teacher threw me in the deep end and expected me to get on with it. Only recently my cousin told me her version of events. Yes, I was thrown in, but she was also there and suffered the same fate. She remembers the teacher telling us to open our eyes and see the fairies. Why is it that Diana went on to love the water and become a competent swimmer and I have never got over my fear of deep water? And why do I only remember my experience and not that she was there as well?

Earlier swimming life in Port Kembla took place on Metal Manufactures and Perkins beaches, to the east of the current Port Kembla beach. My mother swam there as a child and it's where the first town lifesavers demonstrated their bravery. Rescuing people from the sea was part of Port Kembla life. In 1911, only four years after the Australian Surf Lifesaving Club was formed, the town had its own branch. There is a dramatic account of an early rescue by the town's first volunteer lifesaver,

Jack Shannon, at Metal Manufactures Beach in the 1964 *Gazette*, the Metal Manufactures' magazine:

> Suddenly, above the growing roar of the surf, came a cry for help; it was picked up by a dozen throats and carried shoreward as spray-wet faces, wide-eyed and urgent, bounced the call back through the crowd: 'Someone's swept out to sea!' A small boy at the water's edge turned and raced towards the rocks at the southern end of the beach, waving his arms and shouting: 'Mister Shannon, Mister Shannon quick, someone's gone out!'
>
> Jack Shannon heard the boy coming and rolled easily off the big flat rock where he had been sun-baking and loped along the beach to the main surfing area. Pausing a moment to locate the exhausted swimmer, Shannon bounded into the shallows, speared through a breaking wave and thrust out powerfully across the heavy surf to effect yet another single-handed rescue off the M.M. beach.[1]

Jack Shannon, who worked at Metal Manufactures, set standards of bravery, efficiency and self-sacrifice. The only drowning fatality that occurred during his time as lifesaver was during a day when he was not in the area. Decades later, on 30 August 1941, a member of the Port Kembla Surf Lifesaving

Club dived into the sea off Honeycomb Rocks on Red Point to rescue a boy who had been swept out to sea. The lifesaver swam 250 yards (228 metres) to reach and support him until someone brought out a small boat which was then rowed three miles (4.8 kilometres) to safety through treacherous seas. The lifesaver was Norm Emmett and the 14-year-old boy was Doug Shannon, Jack Shannon's 14-year-old son.

In 1912 Metal Manufactures Beach was an exciting place to be when the town's surf club staged its first carnival. The locals easily dominated competition against visiting clubs from Wollongong, Thirroul, Manly and Freshwater. For those who came to watch there was something for everyone: alarm and reel races, rescue and resuscitation, chariot, wheelbarrow and potato sack races – a typical Port Kembla celebration.

As the years went on the initial spirit of vigilance waned and it became difficult to continue to provide beach patrols, but Charlie Jackson was there to help. He organised a group of scouts to run voluntary weekend beach patrols, which breathed new life into the town's surf lifesaving movement.

For 35 years MM Beach was the focus of town beach life. Those who dared go over the hill and swim at the big beach to the south were called 'five-mile boneheads'. But all that changed when the Port Kembla Olympic swimming pool opened there in 1937. The sustained hullabaloo and money spent was enough to shift the focus. The surf club yielded, transferring its services to the beach beside the pool. In 1941 a Port Kembla team won the branch surf teams' championship and in 1956, with help from Mr LF White, general manager of Metal Manufactures, who initiated and guided the project, a new surf pavilion was opened overlooking the beach.

Many said that on 9 February 1963 the most successful surf championship in the history of the Australian Surf Lifesaving Association was held at Port Kembla beach. There were 2,000 competitors, 9,000 spectators, 48 march-past teams, 50 surf boats, and the presence of royal personages and important dignitaries: Prince Richard, son of the Duke and Duchess of Gloucester, accompanied by the Governor of New South Wales, His Excellency Lieutenant-General Sir Eric Woodward and Lady Woodward, along with Judge Adrian Curlewis, national president of the Surf Lifesaving Association. Port Kembla was top of the beach pinnacle, establishing the beach as one of the country's best.[2]

Although industry was our fathers' workplace, the natural world, not just the beaches, was our childhood medium. We were at home in long grass, playing hide and seek, climbing trees. My friends and I were agile, adventurous, sliding down sand dunes and exploring disused quarries. Building dams across creeks on regular weekend picnic outings with my family was a favourite pastime. Outside, not inside, was where my friends and I were happiest.

## 19

# 1950s and the outside world

In the 1950s we were self-contained but not forgotten on our promontory. Drivers heading south needed to come via Five Islands Road and Wentworth Street on their way to Shellharbour. The town was on the road to everywhere, travellers topped up the tills and kept shopkeepers happy, but not for long. In 1956 engineers blasted King Street out of the rock, providing a shortcut south. Drivers now went directly to Warrawong and Lake Illawarra, bypassing Port Kembla completely.

For the first ten years of my life, if the family needed to go anywhere local we walked; to get to more distant places there was the bus or the train. When I was ten my father bought a Morris Oxford, which looked like a black beetle. For the first time in our lives we were free to go anywhere we liked on a sudden whim. We loved Sunday drives – Doug, resisting the urge to go mine-hunting, took us to hidden creeks where we picnicked and paddled. David and I would dam up pools while Audrey and Doug chatted in the shade. Minnamurra Falls, Foxground, Jamberoo, forested escarpments, deep-green fields sloping towards the sea and dotted with dozy cows are imprinted on my mind.

One day in early autumn 1953 I was collected from school and our family drove to Adelaide, where my grandmother lived. It took three days and nights with stops at hotels and the homes of relatives who lived on the way. I understood for the first time where I lived in relation to the rest of the country. We left the coast and travelled into a landscape of brown fields, grey sheep and scraggly gums. There were days and days of it with only hotel stops for relief at places like Hay and Wangaratta. My mother worried about our manners in the middle of nowhere. Dressed in our best we'd sit up with double damask napkins on our laps eating minted lamb. We liked staying with my aunt and uncle in Moe, where my uncle was a bank manager, because there were three cousins to play with.

At the end of the long journey were aunts, uncles and cousins and a large garden with grape vines and almond trees heavy with nuts to crack. One time after my brother and I had filled a large jar with almonds to take home, my grandmother pleaded that we leave a few behind for her. She lived in a stone house in Woodville with a cellar full of preserves and ginger beer. At the large dining table in a room lined with bookcases we ate more roast lamb followed by caramelised apple turnover. Great aunts Vi and Ruby, each the height of ten-year-old me, whirled around calling, 'Who am I? Who am I?'

If we weren't going to Adelaide, holidays were simple affairs. Mostly our family spent the long, seemingly interminable Christmas holidays at home. Sometimes we went with friends to Mossy Point on the South Coast near Nowra. Our parents were happy and we were too, playing in rock pools during the day and at board games at night. One time, my father, David and I went to Christians Minde on Jervis Bay, the first guest house on the far South Coast. We'd sit for hours in a green painted boat on the river with fishing lines dangling. There my father was the most relaxed I'd ever seen him, away from the demands of the coke ovens. Audrey didn't come, it wasn't her scene. Instead she would make one of her visits to cousin Irma in Melbourne and bring back presents like the miniature white china dogs which I still have.

We had little understanding of how isolated we were in the 1950s. There was no 24-hour news cycle or internet connection and no television until midway through the decade. Information trickled in via newspapers, radio, or the newsreels that preceded feature movies at the cinema. We wrote letters to keep in touch and had pen friends. For many years I wrote to a Finnish girl called Pirjo. Once she sent me a 45-rpm vinyl record and I imagined her world of forests and snow as I listened to the music.

We weren't completely isolated – the regular short trip to Wollongong had always been a necessary part of our lives. From the beginning of Port Kembla's history there was constant traffic, first in horse-drawn vehicles and by my time in green double-decker buses, many of them full of high school students. As teenagers we spent hours on the buses, living our lives vicariously as we watched older girls chatting up boys. There was no high school in Port Kembla until 1961. Wollongong was also where we went to buy exotic merchandise and, by the mid-1950s, to hang out in coffee lounges like Hella's Keller and eat foreign food. Hella's Keller was a dark place; you stumbled into low, spongy seats and drank bitter coffee, thinking 'This is the life.'

Our life of disconnectedness was about to end. During the fifties strangers began walking down my street, strangers with different features to ours. My friends and I thought they were aliens and followed them on our bikes. When we saw them finish their journey at the new hostel in Berkeley, greeted by wives and children much like those we knew, it was a let-down. As we heard other languages, shops began selling different food, and our mothers, with the help of the *Women's Weekly*, mastered spaghetti bolognese, it slowly dawned on us we'd been living in a vacuum. The newcomers were mostly from the Mediterranean and the Balkans, looking for work and willing to do jobs rejected by locals in the town's heavy industry. Many of them were Macedonians, arriving through the 1950s and into the 1960s and 1970s in large numbers. Whole villages, such as Bitola, migrated. Faded Cyrillic writing can still be seen today on shopfronts in Wentworth Street. In the 1970s Macedonians made up 55 per cent of the town's population, but I had little to do with them as a child. Now I'm curious about their lives and on one of my return journeys to Port Kembla I notice that the Presbyterian church, where I'd learnt to foxtrot as a teenager during Friday night socials under the benign eye of Reverent Boyle, is now St Kliment Ohridski and painted white. It's an active church community still, evidenced in 2011 when they built a golden dome for the seven-storey bell tower of the monastery overlooking Kembla Grange race course. It took three men ten weeks and the bell tower is said to be the largest in the world. When Bishop Peter came to bless the church, 10,000 Macedonians came to celebrate.[1] They're hoping the complex will become a tourist attraction. These people look after their own: today there's a welfare centre in Port Kembla which provides respite day care, help with language difficulties, ageing issues, and specialised services for Macedonians not provided by the wider community. They also have a quarterly magazine, *Kompas*, and a Macedonian program on community radio.

## Big shots come to town

Not just people looking for work but big shots came to town in the 1950s. When Robert Menzies, the prime minister, arrived to pull the starter lever which began production at the new hot strip mill in 1955, we knew the town had become a focal point. The water tanks, roofs and fences of Australia are made here and I was present at the beginning. I was 11 and have never forgotten the mounds of party food spread along the production line where rolled strips of steel would later cool: cakes made with layers of hazelnut puree and chocolate ganache, little tarts and melt-in-the-mouth meringues flown in specially from Switzerland. Up to then passionfruit sponges and pavlovas had been the fanciest we knew, not complicated layered creations tasting of alcohol. I ate what I could, unconcerned about important people or opening ceremonies. I remember the first red hot strip appearing, probably at a later date, as they couldn't have possibly cleared the cakes and got the whole enterprise rolling the same day.

It's a wonder Robert Menzies returned to our town considering his reception during the wharfies' dispute. On 15 November 1938, at Port Kembla's No. 4 jetty, 180 wharfies refused to load pig iron onto the English tramp steamer the *Dalfram*, which was bound for Kobe in Japan. Ted Roach, head of the Waterside Workers Federation (WWF), who'd won concessions from management regarding rosters and other matters, marshalled his men into a disciplined group and stood firm: the pig iron would be used to make munitions at a time when Japan was engaged in military expansion. BHP compounded the situation by putting off men, complaining the wharfies' dispute was hurting business. By the time Attorney-General Menzies arrived, everyone was cranky. In the crowd that day was Mrs Gwendoline Croft, a member of the women's relief committee who was furious because she'd seen the suffering of many families. 'Pig Iron Bob,' she called out in derision and the name stuck. Ted Roach enjoyed the irony of the day when he and his men were asked to clear a path through the protestors so Menzies could depart. He scoffed, 'Menzies, number one Red-baiter, had to be protected by a communist.' Aware many workers and their families were reaching the end of their endurance during the *Dalfram* dispute, Roach and his men agreed to a compromise. They would move the pig iron if it was the last to be sent to Japan. The cargo was finally loaded onto the *Dalfram* on 24 January 1939. History suggests the dock workers got it right and government and big business, terribly wrong.[2]

## Enriching the Anglo mix

Creative people have always had an affinity with the area – composers, violinists, pianists, sculptors and artists have come from and still live in Port Kembla and the Illawarra. Is it something to do with the tension between the industrial infrastructure and the natural beauty of sea and mountains which stimulates the imagination? Or did the influx of migrants in the 1950s bring with them a range of new cultural practices? Or was it that the children of men working in heavy industry wanted a different life from their fathers? I talked to two people hoping to find out.

Concert pianist Gerard Willems arrived from the Netherlands when he was 12 and lived with his family in a migrant camp in the area. He said, 'Thank God they had the ABC concerts, they were a wonderful release from camp life. I remember Charles Mackerras, Isador Goodman. We had dinner with Alfred Brendel and Nikolayeva and afterwards went back to the camp. It was two extreme ends of the spectrum.

'I had long hair and everyone else had short hair. I wore tight pants and everyone else wore baggy ones. The headmaster thought I was a recalcitrant and against the school rules. That's how he presented me to the other students. Later he followed my career.'

Music would be Gerard's escape. A turning point was hearing Beethoven's *'Moonlight Sonata'* on the radio after the death of his father. He remembers wishing it would go on forever. He would go on to record all 32 of Beethoven's sonatas. Recently at a Government House concert for Governor David Hurley and his staff he told the audience:

'I saw it was not such a bad country. From restriction and negativity came freedom.'

Port Kembla industry is also responsible for musician Michael Fix and his family living in Australia. They came from Germany, his metallurgist father attracted by the work opportunities. When I first heard Michael's song 'Copper Town Blues' on YouTube I was amazed – not only did I like the song, but it was about Port Kembla. Michael sings and plays guitar, and the subject of the song is the demolition of the ER&S stack:

*There's a hole in the ground where the chimney stood*
*and a phantom in the sky*
*See my daddy was a copper man and a company man I guess.*

I get in touch and he's happy to talk. He has positive memories of school, though he does remember falling off the monkey bars and being slapped over the knuckles and called a 'bloody idiot' by a teacher. With friends he spent a lot of time hiding at the edge of the school, waving and calling out to train drivers to blow their horns as they drove past on their way to ER&S. He found the industrial world exciting. With his father he remembers enjoying visits to the ER&S laboratory and recreation room where there were pool tables.

I asked him when he started playing guitar. He said his father owned a guitar but didn't play much and Michael wasn't particularly interested until, aged 11, he heard what he calls the new music: the Top 40 on radio station 2SM. The 1970s and the rise of the singer–songwriter created exciting possibilities for him. Manfred Rentz, a Port Kembla friend whose family also came from Germany, inspired him to write 'Copper Town Blues'. As a child Manfred had lived on Wentworth Street and remembers seeing what he thought was snow falling as it did in his homeland. He ran outside to find that instead of snow it was white ash covering everything – fallout from the nearby works.

Michael explained how the song was written. Another friend, Mark Krail (not from Port Kembla), wrote the lyrics. In 2014 Michael and Manfred bombarded him with their memories and Mark scribbled them down. Later he shaped them into what became the words of 'Copper Town Blues' and Michael wrote the music. The song is included in his album '*Lines and Spaces*' and dedicated to the people of Port Kembla. Michael is one of the world's leading acoustic guitarists and has won three Golden Guitar awards. He's released 13 albums and along with composing, singing and playing guitar, gives guitar workshops and tours widely, particularly in Germany, Italy, the Netherlands and Austria. Port Kembla is where it all began.

The children of these migrant metallurgists, often with vastly different interests from their fathers, have enriched our world.

20

# 1950s: Stand-out events

On an overcast Thursday, 11 February 1954, with a stiff southerly blowing, 13,000 washed and ironed school children from 130 schools assembled in the Wollongong Showground and I was one of them. We waited in lines, fizzing with expectation. At 2.30 p.m. we heard distant cheering, then there she was, Queen Elizabeth II, standing in a slow-moving open car with Prince Philip by her side. We rushed to the fence, ignoring teachers' orders, squeezing together to get a better look. Dressed in grey silk, a small hat hugging her head and rows of pearls round her neck, she was tiny and beautiful. She smiled her smile and waved and we screamed our admiration – she was our rock star. Margaret Buttel, school captain of Wollongong High, spoke for all of us in her speech of welcome, not that we could hear, what with the cheering and buffeting wind. The first reigning monarch to visit Australia, crowned only three years before, was just 12 kilometres away from our town.

Many years later, it's hard to believe the hysteria. Commentators called it the biggest day in Wollongong's history. Towns were disappointed to be left off the royal itinerary.

People gathered at Dunmore House near Shellharbour based on a rumour the Queen was visiting, only to be disappointed. Buses brought people to Wollongong from Milton, Nowra and Mittagong. The whole population turned out to wave what they had: flags or umbrellas in the overcast weather. They cheered as horses pranced either side of the royal open car. Shopkeepers decorated their premises, which were closed for the day. The mayor, JJ Kelly, was dressed for the occasion in ermine and medals. Along the route returned servicemen and women stood in their special places. Five hundred of them, with decorations blazing, formed a guard of honour at the Returned Soldiers Memorial Hall, where the official lunch was held. I wonder what they ate and what the royal couple thought during that day of heightened emotion in an outpost of empire.

The Wollongong Theatre's 35-mm film of the event describes the servicemen as soldiers of the Queen, and much of the coverage emphasised this connection. We in the Illawarra were loyal, fighting for Britain in three wars – the Boer War and the First and Second World Wars. Our family understood this loyalty as one had answered the call for the First World War. The visit was our chance as ordinary citizens of the South Coast to show allegiance and we threw ourselves into it. Union Jack flags decorated the Memorial Hall, not Australian ones – we were still living at home with the British family in 1954 and had no intention of cutting the umbilical cord.[1] The fervour to see the Queen was understandable before television or the internet. We knew if we didn't see her in person, there'd be only newspaper pictures or black and white newsreels to look at.

Times are different now and it seems absurd that we aren't a republic. However, when I visit Parliament House in Canberra and see William Dargie's 1954 painting of Elizabeth II, an intense emotion rushes back. She is fairytale beautiful in her mimosa tulle gown with wattle motifs. Only princesses wear diamond tiaras and necklaces of diamond flowers. The Queen liked the portrait so much she asked for a copy. In drab, badly dressed Australia of the 1950s this vision in yellow took our collective breath away. She wore the dress only twice, on her first official engagement in Sydney and on her last in Perth. Not only was she our queen, she brought glamour to our pre-television lives.

Unlike the Queen, television came directly to our town, to the electrical and white goods supplier in Wentworth Street, to be precise. Shortly before Christmas 1956 my family walked the kilometre to the main street and watched the first black and white images captured on bulky sets. With others we jostled outside the window and couldn't get enough of the flickering life. It was hard to believe you could have this in your own home and turn entertainment on and off when desired.

The first televisions were treated with respect. I remember sitting in front of old Mrs Pratt's – she was also the owner of the town's first car, bought in the early 1900s. Children were welcome, but we were asked to sit quietly on the floor – no eating or drinking and in absolute darkness. Much of the time there was nothing more than a test pattern and we quickly lost interest. By 1957 our family had a set and we no longer sat near the radio listening to *The Argonauts* or *Blue Hills* while my mother knitted, but lounged, soaking up American shows like *Leave It to Beaver, I Love Lucy* and the *Popeye* cartoons. We were relieved to be no longer alone at the end of the world and our preoccupation with all things American began. With heads full of the American lives acted out on our TV screens night after night, we were conditioned to believe this was the new norm and everything British, including the Queen, became old hat.

21

# 1960s: Exodus

In spite of my family's long association with the town, by the 1960s my parents and others like them began looking for a new place to live. It was the quality of the air that sent them packing. What brought prosperity also brought pollution and those who could, retreated to the rainforest belt along the escarpment behind Wollongong. The irony is that the people responsible for creating the pollution were the first to leave. My parents' choice was Mount Keira, where they built a house on Steelworks' land that had been released to senior staff for purchase. Audrey grew the garden she'd always wanted full of bluebells and camellias, and Doug planted his maples. My father drove each day to the coke ovens and returned in the evening to his plot of bush with its fast-running creek. I wondered when it began to dawn that Port Kembla's air was affecting people's health, and found a 1948 letter to the editor of the *Illawarra Mercury*:

> Dear Sir
>
> I was pleased to note in a recent copy of your paper a letter by a Port Kembla citizen protesting

against the smoke nuisance caused by the large chimney of ER&S. I am a new resident in the district and one who has considered buying here. However, I would not like to permanently reside in an area whose air was constantly polluted by the fumes from that stack, nor would I raise a family here.

Apparently despite the labour shortages and the importance of Port Kembla as an industrial area the authorities, be they council or industry, do not sincerely want people to settle here. Fortunately there are other places on the South Coast where land is available and the air is fresh.

Yours etc.

Gasping[1]

Is Gasping right? Were authorities not interested in dealing with the issue? Or was the pollution problem simply too hard to solve? Port Kembla people had put up with it for years as a necessary by-product of financial security, and unfortunately those who stayed endured chronic health problems. My Port Kembla primary school classmate, Helen Hamilton, said in an ABC interview, 'I forever had colds, bronchitis and sinus stuff like that when I was young. You just had to learn by suffering. Don't open the windows today!'

Eric Eklund in his book *Steel Town: The making and breaking of Port Kembla*, blames the town's decline on transport changes and the building of a major supermarket in Warrawong.

From my observation those with financial means —doctors, dentists, shop owners, accountants, works managers, engineers and metallurgists – left in the late 1950s and early 1960s, not for shopping or transport reasons, but because they were seeking cleaner air. Port Kembla's professional residents moved away in one go, which didn't help local businesses. The town's run of prosperity was over and with the exodus, businesses closed. By 1966 there were 26 vacant shops. Over time, sellers of drugs and their associates, including prostitutes, moved in to fill the vacuum. The decline continued into the 1970s, and the 1980s and 1990s were a down time for the town.

Not only Port Kembla people were aware of the pollution problem. In 1954, the *Newcastle Herald and Miners Advocate* reported Mr Sullivan from the State Health Department saying: 'Port Kembla suffered greater atmospheric pollution than Newcastle or Sydney.'

Pressure was building. In 1959 Dr Alan Bell conducted a study of 947 Port Kembla residents and found they had higher levels of mild chronic bronchitis compared with his Corrimal control group. Bell attributed these findings to the sulphur dioxide gas in the atmosphere. The results of this study and the concerted efforts of Rex Connor, State member for Wollongong–Port Kembla, and others, forced the New South Wales Parliament to pass the *Clean Air Act* in 1961, the first major legislative response to industrial pollution in Australia.

Action was needed in the town and everyone knew the answer – a stack. For years ER&S management had been talking about building a bigger chimney to replace the original one. Mr Porter, the member for Wollongong in the New South Wales Legislative Assembly, stated in 1964, 'The construction of the ER&S Stack, one of the tallest chimneys in the world, is the first fruits of the *Clean Air Act* introduced by the State Australian Labor Party.'

In 2014, just before its demolition, the *Illawarra Mercury* asked the men responsible for building the stack how they felt. The engineer, Boyd Thompson said, 'I don't want to get involved in "for" and "against". I just want to pay tribute to ER&S who had the courage to spend the money under difficult circumstances to build the chimney. The company honestly did believe they were doing the right thing at the time for the area.'[2]

The building of the stack was a major undertaking for the firm. As far back as 1959 the *Illawarra Mercury* was reporting: 'At ER&S there are plans under consideration for the building of a new and higher stack or other means of rendering the gases innocuous.'[3] Before the decision to build, a variety of other ways of dispersing gases was considered. Those in charge knew there was no point transferring the problem from Park Street to Primbee – a suburb a few kilometres away. New gas collection systems were investigated, but with tons of emissions spewing out every day it was impossible to collect and convert them all into fertiliser. They tried installing a new sinter plant in 1959 and replacing the old Pierce Smith converters with new larger converters. With little reduction of pollution from these measures the bosses realised the only solution for dispersal and dilution of emissions was to build a taller stack. It was not a straightforward process as Wollongong Council delayed construction due to zoning regulations. Because of the importance of the venture the State Labor government under Bob Heffron intervened and overturned the council's objections.

Building began on the site of the smelter manager's residence in 1963. It cost $400,000 ($5 million today) and when finished was the tallest stack in the Southern Hemisphere. It took truckloads of materials, two years and many men to build. Tileman and Company of Melbourne were the construction company, utilising 2000 cubic yards of concrete, 100 tons of reinforcing steel and 220,000 bricks. The concrete lining foundations were 85 feet (26 metres) in diameter and the chimney was 10 feet (3 metres) thick. (Hence the amount of dynamite needed to blow it up in 2014.) It was greeted with enthusiasm from the locals when it was finished. 'Landmark Completed' was the *Illawarra Mercury* headline in 1965:

> A Scotsman and a part Aboriginal, Bryan Mongta, tugged a string to mark the completion of the ER&S Company's sky-scraping stack on Friday. A pale green flag fluttered to the top of a mast and three cheers echoed from about a dozen representatives of ER&S and the Tileman Construction company who were bracing themselves against a 40-knot wind. Site foreman Tony Boland said he chose Bryan to assist in the historic task of raising the Tileman flag because he had been a good worker on the job.[4]

At the time the stack appeared to solve the pollution problem. According to a report by the Director General of Public Health issued later in 1965, 'tests made during the summer have shown it to be completely effective'. My uncle, Harry Hartley, was general manager of ER&S during the chimney's construction and the stack came to be known as Hartley's Folly. Hard-working Harry went straight to ER&S from school and studied accountancy at night. Several nights a week he did the books for Port Kembla hotels, making the extra money needed to send his children to boarding school. He was at ER&S all his working life, rising to general manager, a position he found lonely at times, according to his daughter Diana. He was the family success story. His father Alfred had started as an accountant at ER&S and finished as a departmental manager. His brother Leigh, and sisters Hazel and Audrey also worked there for a short time while Harry rose to be the boss. Sadly he didn't have much time to enjoy the fruits of his success, dying at 64 from an aortic aneurysm.

ER&S wasn't the only offender when it came to pollution in Port Kembla. Steelmaking had many noxious gases formed as by-products of production and the culprit at the coke ovens was benzene. Even though it was known that benzene was a hematological toxin, according to the *Illawarra Mercury*, 'BHP denied the gas link to leukaemia'. Not until September 1996 was the monitoring of benzene begun. Mike Head writes in *Cancer and Industrial Pollution* (1996):

> That was when information made public by one young leukaemia victim, Melissa Cristiano, forced the Carr New South Wales Government and the Illawarra Public Health Unit to reveal the leukaemia epidemic among young people in areas close to the works.[5]

Whether cancer clusters were a coincidence or due to local environmental conditions or a combination of both is hard to prove. But those who stayed in the town and surrounding areas had a higher incidence of certain diseases than elsewhere. They paid a price for Port Kembla's industrial prosperity; others, like my family, got out before it was too late.

The paradox is that when the town was full of pollution, it was full of life. Now with the stack demolished, ER&S, Metal Manufactures and Australian Fertilisers closed and the air clean, the town is empty. Clean air has come at a price. Today, industries have more or less left the town and the actions of those that remain are scrutinised by newly confident local pollution watchdogs.

I have come to appreciate my memories of the 1950s town. The main street full of shops, the library stocked with books. There were tennis courts to play on, churches with active congregations, friends to play with and many families like mine whose fathers worked in the industries. We noticed the pollution but weren't fully aware of the threat to health. Suddenly, like lemmings, instead of following each other over a cliff, we left in a swarm for less polluted places. Those who were less financially mobile stayed and put up with it, enduring suspicious clusters of health problems. Going back, I see what upset me as a child and what the white blow-ins with power had missed: the fragility and beauty of the place. Heavy industry was the last thing this landscape needed.

Wentworth Street in 2017

PART TWO

# Rediscovery and Reconnection

## 22

# 2014: Demolition day

End or new beginning – what's it to be? Everywhere you look in Port Kembla there are rusting sheds and overgrown industrial sites. Now the ER&S Stack, the copper chimney locals call the Giant Cigarette, once the Southern Hemisphere's tallest smoke stack, is scheduled for demolition, and reporters from the *Illawarra Mercury* have the action covered:

'It's a sore point for me. It'll be upsetting to watch and might bring tears to my eyes,' says pub patron John McDonald, who is in town for the event.

Another upset drinker suggests, 'Nobody will ever be able to find Port Kembla again.'

Maybe he's right. Becalmed on its point, surrounded by sea, islands and beaches, its ageing Steelworks still puffing smoke occasionally, there's a whiff of abandonment about the town. Yet it generates strong feelings in its residents. There's no way most of them will miss this event. Early on the morning of 20 February 2014 anticipation builds. Men take time off work. The Port Kembla Steelworks Hotel, built in 1890 at the northern end of town and known as Top Pub, has a clear view of the action. It's just outside the exclusion zone and will act as a beery gathering point. Adam Moxton explains why he's here.

'I'm reminiscing with my old mates remembering the days when the glitter would fall from the stack in the playground at school.'[1]

Pieta Grinrod, the proprietor, is hoping hundreds, maybe thousands will join them for a free barbeque and has prepared special cocktails.

'They're blue, green, red and meant to look a bit like the stack.'[2]

Others, like Helen Hamilton, who campaigned long and hard to have it demolished, are glad the day has come and are staying away, wary of possible sinister substances in the fallout dust. As far as she's concerned, they've lived far too long with industrial pollution. She tells an ABC reporter:

'We had a vegetable garden and my dad would sometimes tell my mum not to touch the stuff in the garden because they let the arsenic out last night.'[3]

Like it or not, for nearly 50 years it had given locals their bearings – even acting as a marine navigation tool for fishermen and sailors and guiding cars home from Stanwell Tops or Robertson up on the escarpment. In the 1950s with no stack we accepted pollution as a necessary by-product of industrial prosperity. When it was built residents were persuaded by the company spiel that the stack improved air quality by moving smoke higher into the atmosphere. But no longer: false starts, stays of action and 11 years of debate are over and the skyline of Port Kembla is to be altered forever – the giant puffer of toxins is coming down.

The group which calls itself 'Stack 360' did its best to save it. Just weeks before demolition, using swirling coloured lights and sound, they promoted the stack as a focus of entertainment. The group was hoping to persuade those in charge of its tourist potential. But no, the new Japanese owners, ignoring talk of heritage and using the spectre of concrete cancer to justify their actions, have forged ahead with their plans.

At 7.30 a.m. on the day, 20 February 2014, 250 residents are evacuated from the 300-metre exclusion zone. Hard to believe that in a matter of minutes this landmark will be obliterated. Although police are on duty and barricades are in place, there's a carnival atmosphere. Families watch from nearby Gallipoli Park with binoculars focused and picnics ready for later. Mobile phones, fancy cameras on tripods and air-born ones in hovering helicopters are primed, making sure the moment is captured, over and over.

Time moves slowly. It's up to the experts now, a precision explosion is what they want. Preparation is intense and has taken three years to fine-tune. Rumours of asbestos abound. No, says Ian Wilson, the general manager of Port Kembla Copper, the company who now owns the stack, all has been resolved. He reassures locals the site is clear and the stack's central tunnels where asbestos was found have been removed. Samples of the 7,000 tons of bricks, concrete and steel have been tested and the results were negative. Early morning, explosives the size of sausages are inserted into holes at the northern side of the base of the stack. Detonators are attached which will communicate with the firing system and on explosion create a wedge ensuring the stack falls in the right direction. According to Ian Wilson, 'The top part can't fall fast enough to keep up with the bottom, so it's likely to split into two or three. It will fall broadly to the north.'[4]

PKC suggests several possible morning explosion times. The town waits – but not until after 11 a.m. are the 934 charges detonated. There's a loud, muffled boom and for a moment, undecided, looking like a giant rocket, the stack rests on its dust cushion before slowly falling sideways and breaking into two pieces between two empty industrial buildings, just as planned. As it lands there's a noise like huge waves hitting rocks. The precision is astounding. People cheer and raise cans of beer for the cameras as putrid dust falls back over the town in one last polluting gasp. The felling of the stack is momentarily upstaged by a man wearing a shirt and nothing else who gets into the frame of the Channel Nine broadcast. Afterwards I experience the event over and over on YouTube – I can't get enough!

Everyone gets into the act. The *Illawarra Mercury* seizes a money-making opportunity, selling blue and white 'Fall of an Icon' T-shirts, the 'I' in the shape of the stack, for $25. Local business identities and politicians are happy to utilise the event for their own purposes, labelling it symbolic. They're in a hurry to move on and forget the town's contentious industrial past and there's no better way to mark this new order than with a spectacular demolition! The razing becomes an instant hit on social media and Michael Fix's song 'Copper Town Blues' immortalised the stack's demise.[5]

Demolition of Port Kembla Stack, 20 February 2014 (Peter Gilmore)

# 23 Women of the Port

Fifty-six years after leaving Port Kembla as a child, I'm back and exhilarated by what I'm finding. Today is a clear autumn day after a week of stormy weather, and I have a meeting with Jenny Briscoe-Hough at the community centre. When I arrive Jenny is watching what is happening out the window. Police, a man and a woman, are talking to a young woman and Jenny is worried because the woman's reactions are often aggressive. When all seems right we sit to talk and I comment on how impressed I am by Lynn Walworth's film *Tender*, about the plans for a local funeral parlour. Lynn is a close friend of my friend Jenny Sages, who had taken me to see some of Lyn's installations at Sydney's Carriage Works.

I discuss with Jenny how I want to weave my family's history and Port Kembla's together, emphasising early twentieth century life. I tell her I've already written a large chunk of what I know and now it's time to ask others for their memories. I talk about my shame at the way Aboriginal people were treated in the early years.

Jenny says, 'What I've learnt from conversations is the biggest barrier for honest discourse is white people's lack of connection with the land.' She also says, 'We must let Aboriginal people deal with their issues in their own way, but we need to foster relationships and try to understand them better.'

She gives me a list of women who are passionate about Port Kembla and notes that being bolshie is one of their recurring characteristics. I say I can be bolshie when I have to, otherwise I wouldn't have lasted teaching at an all-boys school. While Jenny and I are talking, a man, minus most of his teeth, comes into the office looking for a syringe.

I have come to Port Kembla with my friends Jan and Robert, and after my meeting at the community centre we drive to the inner harbour. Jan takes photos of the old industrial buildings – faded red and atmospheric. Huge cranes form a still-life along the disused wharf and two men are fishing nearby. We return to Wentworth Street for lunch at the Red Point Cafe. Robert goes to withdraw money and on his return tells us he was propositioned. According to him it was all in the look, no words are said. We laugh, not really believing him. I learn later that several of the girls specialise in servicing older men. At the cafe, Kathyrn Orton, Robert and Jan's artist friend, introduces us to Dulcie Dal Molin, who later shows us old Port photos which she has restored to look like the originals. I see Wentworth Street as it was the day the photo was taken, a huddle of buildings not yet a town.

We drive up the hill to my old street. This time I'm OK about time moving on and my house not being there, but can't quite accept that my cousin's house, which seemed substantial in the 1950s, is now past its prime. I remember parties there when I was 14 and how ill-at-ease I felt because I didn't know anyone. My aunt, a lover of the social life, organised us into tennis games during the day and dressed-up events at night. There were coloured lights in the trees, party food laid out on tables and we jived around self-consciously.

This time in town I find I'm less preoccupied with what isn't here, and more interested in the present and planned future changes. I notice the place feels livelier and there are more cars in Wentworth Street. Jenny B-H says there is definitely a resurgence happening but some of the new people aren't keen on a warts-and-all Port Kembla – they want it sanitised.

***

It's autumn 2015 and I'm overwhelmed by the women I meet on this visit who are positive about the future, even though, like social worker Sheryl Wiffin, they have also experienced Port Kembla's dark times. For many years Sheryl has worked at the Community Centre as a drug and alcohol counsellor, and I get from her a sense of the downward spiral after my family left in 1959. The 1960 opening of the Lake Market Shopping Centre in Warrawong sapped the life out of the town, followed by a Big W Store in 1965, then David Jones. The Westfield Group took over the complex in 1985. All this, on top of the building of the King Street bypass in 1956, was the final straw for Wentworth Street.

Sheryl tells me the 1990s were a sad time. The street was dying, businesses left one by one and shopfronts were boarded up. Local authorities turned away, lavishing their attention on more prosperous areas. Port Kembla always had a shady side, as do most seaports but, according to Sheryl, it was never as bad as the newspapers reported: 'Everywhere needs a scapegoat and Port Kembla is that for the Illawarra.'

With shops shut, drug dealers and prostitutes using abandoned buildings, and five pubs and one club fully operational, it's no wonder my 80-year-old mother was horrified when she came on a Sunday afternoon drive-through with my father at that time. Sheryl describes some of the challenges of the 1990s: HIV, gaining the trust of the working girls who feared they would be busted, and starting a clean syringe program. The increased number of boarding houses in Port Kembla compared with other areas was one reason for the higher level of mental health issues.

Things were about to change. Wollongong Council could no longer ignore complaints from residents who wanted sex workers and drug dealers gone. In 2000 Darcy House was established at 1 Old Port Road, giving the sex workers somewhere to go during the day and, from the community's perspective, taking them off the streets. There were fridges full of food, washing machines, showers, lockers and people to talk to.

According to Sheryl, believing in a new Port Kembla was difficult for some. They thought it was because of the sex workers that the town had gone to the dogs. She liked the

Holland model and used it when establishing Darcy House as a drop-in centre. As she said, 'There will always be poor and unfortunate people and we should be doing more to help them.' She was the only paid staff member at that time and said the experience nearly killed her. These days Sheryl has moved on to the community centre at the other end of town and Darcy House is run by the Baptists as a drop-in centre for homeless and disadvantaged people. But, Sheryl says, men are the ones who mostly use it as the women no longer see it as a place that answers their needs.

She talked of going recently to the latest hot spot in the street and finding syringes, old dirty mattresses and condoms and cleaning it up. She wants the local businesses to lift their game, occupying and developing buildings and bringing new life back to the street. But she also wants the disadvantaged to be cared for with dignity. As Sheryl says, 'If you have never experienced love, you can't love yourself.' I hug her as I leave, emotional and relieved someone is there for these people.

***

At Tonitto Cakes on Wentworth Street, I'm back in my 1950s Port Kembla. My husband, John, is with me and as we enter I see the layers of brightly lit cakes: cannoli, cartocci, biscotti, vanilla slices, ricotta cakes, eclairs and a special display of celebratory constructions piled high with cream. When we walk later along the old MM Beach to the abandoned rock pool and marvel at the crisp clean air, the seascape and the benign shapes of industry behind us, I have a Rip Van Winkle experience: how have the old polluting industries of my childhood been transformed into something that looks like a Jeffrey Smart painting?

On this visit we're staying at Sadie's B and B in Keira Street. It's on the hill where I lived as a child and has a perfect vantage point: from the front garden we can see the chimneys of the Steelworks' coke ovens belching smoke, the two huge cylindrical blast furnaces, the cranes on the harbour and, in the distance, the escarpment with its bulges of Mount Keira and Mount Kembla. To the east the Five Islands are dotted on the sea beneath an ever-changing sky.

In the morning coincidences pile up as I chat with Tim, the musician owner. I tell him that the week before I had been to the Watters Gallery in Sydney and seen paintings of Port Kembla by Evan Salmon.

'He lives next door,' Tim tells us.

'The yellow crane painting was my favourite,' I say.

Tim points to the harbour. 'There it is.'

That's not the end of it. The driver of the crane was Sadie's second husband, who lived in both Evan's and Tim's houses. At 90 Sadie was persuaded by her daughter to sell and move to a retirement home near Hill 60.

The previous afternoon, in rain and squally wind, I'd walked around the corner into Robertson Street. No one was about and I was marooned in childhood. Returning to the physical geography of one's past is unsettling when nothing remains. Looking at the elaborate Italianate house now occupying the site of our modest family home, I struggled to conjure up a sense of living here – my memories seem more real. I walked up Bland Street to my cousin's house, which, although it is still there, is more disconcerting than the absence of mine. I remember it as a glamorous house. Not any longer. A brown caravan is parked on the front lawn and the house needs a coat of paint. Without a garden it's exposed. Through the front window I see a woman ironing in what was my aunt and uncle's old bedroom. I return to Sadie's via the old dunny lane that connects with Keira Street and drive to Wollongong library to view old photos of Port Kembla. I find one of Wentworth Street taken by Frank Hurley in the 1950s. The bumper to bumper VJ Holden cars support my memories of the town as a bustling place.

***

The following day Nella Keenan is the first of three amazing women I meet. Jenny, from the Community Centre, has sent me to talk to her. She is passionate about Port Kembla, watching over it like a benign goddess, pouncing if anything threatens its wellbeing. Her parents migrated from Cassino in Italy, a town that was unlucky to be in the way of several armies over past centuries. The battle at Monte Cassino was responsible for thousands of deaths on both sides in the Second World War and the destruction of much of the old city of Cassino. In 1952 Nella's father and his cousins left and came to Port Kembla. They lived in a rented house in Cowper Street and worked shift work at the Steelworks. Her mother came later, married her father at St Patrick's, and they started life together.

'Dad grew grapes and tomatoes, bought olives to pickle and made his own sausages. Our family of cousins often used to gather to do this. As soon as we could buy them in the shops we stopped. A few years ago we got together again to make a different type of sausage.'

Nella remembers the wonderful smells of Contorino, the delicatessen at the top of Wentworth Street that opened in the 1950s, its narrow space packed with mortadella, olive oil, passata, tinned tuna.

'It was one of the last shops to go, people came from everywhere. On Saturday mornings there were four lines out on to the street, it was chocablock.'

Later Coles and Woolworths opened deli counters to cater for these people who ate a different diet from the one we were used to. Nella went to school in the town and grew up with a mother who spoke her mind. She remembers being embarrassed as a child about being Italian. When she married it never occurred to her she would live anywhere else and she managed to persuade her husband to move from Thirroul and come to Port Kembla. Somewhere along the way she became an activist. She says you have to watch big industry, they do things under the radar and the next thing they are up and running and polluting. She arranged a meeting with Vesuvius, an engineering firm in Port Kembla, because she was not happy with their development. She said to them, 'You need to leave a legacy, we've been lied to, cheated on and polluted on.' Nella got her way, the company agreed to improve the land around their factory, putting in ponds for wildlife and gardens.

I asked what motivated her to take on these people. She wasn't sure but thought her background had made her open to others and their needs. She grew up a Catholic but now calls herself an Evangelical, like her husband. She says if you want culture to change, you have to make it happen: when someone puts trash in the place where you grew up, you have to speak out. She belongs to a core group committed to the future development of Port Kembla and believes the town will have a second wind, noting that real estate prices have gone up and the place is back on people's maps. Nella says Jenny Briscoe-Hough has harnessed the passionate feeling for Port Kembla. Nella sees herself as lucky because she doesn't have a lot of personal baggage and believes in a pyramid of nurture.

'You have to look after yourself first, then your partner, followed by the children and only then can you concentrate on community matters.' It comes as no surprise that she is also a disability support worker. As I leave, Nella presses books on to me to help with my project.

***

Ann Martin is the owner of Sadie's B and B and also a local councillor. She explains the attraction of Port Kembla: 'I like the contrast between natural beauty and industry, it has a powerful energy. Auckland, built on seven volcanoes, has the same energy.' She talks of the challenges. 'Wollongong Council has a historical unwillingness to engage with southern suburbs and the town.'

I think of what Sheryl Griffin said about Port Kembla being an easy place to scapegoat. Working class, multicultural and with active unions, bureaucrats ignored the place. Ann says it was often easier to bypass the council and go to the South Coast Labour Council if you wanted something done.

'There's a long history of activism in Port Kembla. When the shopping centre opened in Warrawong, a group of locals took over the supermarket in Port Kembla and ran it. Activism and looking after Port Kembla's interests continues today with the Billy Cart Derby held each year in the main street, bush care work, urban renewal programs and the cut price funeral project, Tender.'

I'm getting used to meeting women like Ann in this town with their superhuman energy and get-up-and-go attitude. I love the description of her wedding to musician husband Tim a few years ago. They were married opposite the primary school, looking out towards the Five Islands. Ann wore a bright red dress made by Cheboom, one of several wedding shops in Wentworth Street. She says she was channelling her Spanish great-grandmother. The mood at the reception, held in the old National Bank, was flamenco. Tim and his friends organised cabaret-style music. Port Kembla Men's Shed provided pizzas. They cooked them in their ovens at the top of Wentworth Street and ran down the hill to hungry wedding guests. One of Anne's earlier initiatives was the Port Kembla Festival.

'We took over the Star Cafe, known for selling grog and gambling, and ran back-to-back bands for a month. People came from everywhere. It was ahead of its time and proved to me if you have something good, people will come.'

Her current focus is the Old School Project which, if it happens, will be built on the site of my old primary school. It's ambitious and could transform the town. In a complicated manoeuvre, she is negotiating with developers and Port Kembla Copper, who currently own the land. Her vision is to provide studios, workshops and teaching space for artists, turning it into a creative hub, attracting visiting artists from around the world. To pay for this, houses would be built on the other part of the land and sold.

'The Illawarra is transitioning,' says Ann. She wants to attract high technology industries and boutique manufacturing to the area. She's working to bring cruise ships to the Port and imagines a time when tourists will take master classes in painting at the new artists' precinct, learn to surf at the beach or go on trips to the Highlands. She laughs at the thought of Port Kembla as a tourist destination and knows Wollongong people think it's crazy. There are even more adventurous people proposing to build a hotel perched on rocks on the site of the old sewerage treatment works on the point near the beach – during high tides waves would wash over it. Risky ideas have arrived. As well as being a councillor, Ann is a poet, artist and activist and tells me about loving to watch the full winter moon glowing red as it rises over the edge of the sea. She's in tune with the beauty and is on a mission to brings others here.

Ann sends me across Wentworth Street to visit Ambling Home, a shop where used fabrics are turned into something new. Ponchos, pyjamas and skirts are made out of old blankets, sheets and curtains. I meet Amanda, who runs it, and find out she lives in my uncle's old house in Bland Street; the woman I'd seen ironing the night before was her. I mention that my aunt loved entertaining and she said she had sensed that. Even after several changes of owners there was something about the house suggesting a grander past life.

***

From the Seascape Cafe on Foreshore Road I look out to sea towards the Five Islands and the huge container vessels waiting their turn to enter the harbour. Behind them is the escarpment and Mt Keira and in the foreground are the cranes. The 40 white pyramids of the old tank traps are arranged in a pattern on the green grass adjoining the cafe, and are now part of the new Port Kembla Heritage Park. They are as beautiful as any art installation – I'm glad they have survived. I transpose my family's history onto this smartened up, redeveloped site. My mother remembered the first breakwaters being built and strolling down Darcy Road in the evening to view the ships. Now Darcy Road is nothing more than an access road to the port, with abandoned sheds on over-grown lots on either side. My cousins' grandfather, Captain Gordon, was harbour master during the 1920s when it was a port serving the busy industry clustered close by. My father used to take David and me fishing here in the 1950s. We'd drop our lines over the edge of the wharf and wait. The rest of the time we watched the men working on the ships and the comings and goings of sailors. We'd take our fish, usually bream, and give them to Audrey who cooked them reluctantly, as she was not keen on all the gutting and scaling.

***

Helen Hamilton is the fourth activist I meet in 24 hours. She was one of the heroines of the successful fight against Port Kembla Copper's bid to reopen for business in 1997. The *Illawarra Mercury* called her Australia's Erin Brockovich. She's waiting at her front door, a small lady in a zip-up pink fleece, not at all how I'd imagined a person who had taken on the premier of New South Wales. She was in my class at school and I want to understand how she got from there to now.

She says she was thrown in the deep end and laughs because as a child she didn't speak up for herself. But the sight of her granddaughter with acid burns from pollution was too much. It gave her the courage to speak out and join the protest against the town's heavy industry. Like Nella, she attributed her actions to her Christian beliefs: 'God pushed me in the deep end and taught me how to float, walk in deep water and stand up for myself.'

In 1997 the smelting of copper was set to begin again with supposed emission-reducing technology and best-practice environmental controls. The New South Wales government and Premier Bob Carr didn't want to upset the Japanese owners of Port Kembla Copper as their countrymen had weighed in heavily with money for the forthcoming 2000 Olympics.

Furious they hadn't been consulted, Helen and others, including Michael Sergent, a community-minded lawyer, formed a group appropriately named IRATE (Illawarra Residents Against Toxic Emissions). She says Legal Aid was wonderful in helping organise the campaign. They planned to stop the reopening by taking the case to the Land and Environment Court, but to do this they needed a litigant. The company had gone in hard and threatened to sue them if they stopped the smelter. As she had nothing to lose, with no house or job, Helen said she would be that person.[1]

The night before the court case the Carr government passed the Port Kembla Development Bill. Helen said it felt like the day democracy died. Helen and the group weren't finished. Tim Robertson, brother of Geoffrey the human rights barrister, helped them challenge under the Freedom of Information laws to get reports surrounding the health and environmental effects of the reopening of Port Kembla Copper. Helen appeared in court and won. It became a landmark case regarding the release of government information. Helen was feted and asked to talk on advocacy to various groups, including universities. The moment that means the most to her was when she was on a Sydney train, talking to a family from Tasmania. They were up for special medical treatment for their sick daughter and said they were able to access the treatment because of the court's interpretation of the Freedom of Information laws.

As we sit talking, looking at old school photographs, attempting to recognise ourselves, Helen's phone rings constantly. She has a new fight on her hands: truckloads of gypsum were seen being driven up Wentworth Street, even though Port Kembla Milling – the presumed destination – knew it was against the law. She rings a contact there and he refuses to believe her unless she produces photographs to prove it, testing her to the limit. She's expected to be at every rule-breaking event. Helen runs the Port Kembla Pollution Group and says industry constantly flouts the rules. Recently there was a fire in the Sinter Plant which, Helen alleges, was covered up by the Steelworks.

Recently she was involved in a stoush over Hill 60 when developers wanted to build a motel. Helen found old maps of the site to prove Aboriginal occupation, pinpointing where families had lived for thousands of years. She went straight to the Army, who controlled the area, as she no longer trusted governments to have the best interests of the town at heart. She won and the land is now part of a heritage park.

After the controversy generated by Helen and her friends, the reopening of the copper smelter in 2000 was carefully watched. Explosions, gas clouds and fines for non-compliance finally finished off any chance for the plant and it was shut down in 2003. No longer will industry get away with bad polluting practices, not while women like Helen are awake to their shoddy behaviour.

Ignore these women at your peril, I say to any Port Kembla industry planning shady business. I think back to the 1950s and our passive acceptance of Port Kembla as a polluted place. The only way to deal with it was to shut up or get out. I admire Helen for staying and fighting. My family response was to leave. Of my family, only Gertrude and Arthur lived and died there. Their daughter Hazel left in the 1920s to live in England with her twins. Son Leigh, returned from the First World War, moved away to Brisbane with wife Dolly. Harry and Audrey stayed until the 1950s and then both built houses in the lush green escarpment behind Wollongong.

***

On 30 October 2016 Ann Martin's wish was fulfilled. Crowds lined the inner harbour foreshores to watch the first-ever cruise ship arrive. They'd come to celebrate and weren't disappointed. Tug boats sprayed water cannons as the top-heavy *Radiance of the Seas* manoeuvred itself into position at the Port Kembla car cargo berth, its huge white bulk a contrast to the adjacent taupe-coloured industrial infrastructure. The company who owns the ship, Royal Caribbean, says this is not the end of it. *Explorer of the Seas*, one of the world's largest cruise ships, is booked to visit on 13 March 2018. One million dollars a day is the sum purported to be generated by these visits – a significant boost to the town's growing tourist industry.[2]

# 24
# Coomaditchie women

I've come to meet Lorraine Brown at the Coomaditchie Centre. I want to learn about the Indigenous people living here, although I'm hesitant, worrying my questions may be intrusive. As a child growing up here I had no real contact with the Indigenous residents. Loraine appeared in the film *Tender* and impressed me with her confident approach to matters affecting her people. I feel confident she can help me.

Every time I return, the town seems cheerier. I notice early twentieth century buildings I'd missed last time, and the healthy Norfolk Island pine trees which give the main street a tropical, holiday feel. What appeared empty and abandoned on earlier visits now looks peaceful and friendly. Standing in the middle of the road, I take photos of a 1921 butcher shop which is still selling meat. I want to buy a platter I'd seen in a window of a closed second-hand goods shop, but it's still closed. The florist next door says she could have sold everything in the window many times over, especially the harp, however the woman who owns the shop is not interested in selling. The space behind the shop is crammed full of stuff and her children say when she dies they are going to get a dump truck, fill it up and take it to the tip. The florist advises if I get there just before the dump truck arrives I'll get what I want.

I call into the Community Centre and talk to Jenny. Even though I haven't seen her for months she hugs me warmly. 'You've got to finish your project, Pam. You should talk to Anne-Louise Rendal, she's doing an oral history/performance project on Port Kembla.' I ask Jenny about the Tender project. I'd heard from another source that she'd been involved preparing a close friend for burial a few months previously. She tells me the funding has just come through.

As I drive past the Coomaditchie Lagoon on my way to my appointment with Lorraine, pelicans hover before sweeping in for a smooth landing. I think about the specialness of this place and its significance for Indigenous people. I learnt about its importance from Lorraine's video *Coomaditchie*, made as part of the Lake Illawarra MAP (Memory and Place) Project.[1] In it she talks about the vulnerability of this perched dunal lake, the only one remaining in the Illawarra area. Drains full of toxic substances flow into it, people dump goldfish that breed and gobble up the natural reeds, and eastern long-necked tortoises choke on plastic bags. As it's one of the primary breeding grounds for the threatened green and gold bell frog and an important refuge for many birds, including swans and pelicans, it's important Lorraine's voice is heard.

I walk towards the old tennis club building that is now home to the Coomaditchie United Corporation. A group of young women are outside, talking with Sue, the manager. Sue sees me and explains the morning's drama. Lorraine's husband has just had a suspected stroke and Lorraine has rushed home where she is waiting for an ambulance. Sue suggests I talk to the children sitting around a painting table eating chips and bread while she checks the situation. They are welcoming and full of information. I concentrate on working out their family connections. They tell me their names, Toeweakia, Mia and Larni, and explain they are grandchildren of Narelle, Lorraine's sister. They chat about the recent Wollongong Council's Secret Suburbs program where their paintings were displayed. Toeweakia, who is 12, points out her paintings of tortoises and dolphins on the wall for sale. While we talk the children are busy. Mia and Larni are decorating white plastic masks with cobalt blue paint, working happily without supervision. I ask how they start and Toeweakia explains, 'Narelle draws the shapes and we paint over them.'

Mia tells me about riding bikes and the school friends who come to play with her near the lagoon. One time they left rubbish and she asked them to take it away because it was not good for the tortoises. At eight she is taking her custodian role seriously.

An older woman rushes over to give directions to the young women who are working on a canvas. It's Narelle. I want to talk to her but know she has more important things on her mind, but she is gracious and willing to chat while she has lunch. She explains that the canvas is being painted by young medical students from Wollongong University who are here as part of a 'Breaking Down Barriers' program run by the Centre.

They are following a design Narelle has given them, and when it's finished the plan is that the canvas will hang in the Wollongong University School of Medicine. Narelle explains that in painting it they learn about signs and totems and their significance to her people without needing to ask directly. She calls it 'sideways learning'. I notice there are no young men in the group and wonder why.

Narelle tells me how just recently an older Aboriginal woman in a wheelchair was discharged from the local hospital without having transport arranged for her, and sat for hours until somebody realised she'd been abandoned. Narelle sees the problem as lack of respect, which happens regularly. As I sit beside her she tells me that some hospital workers still dislike touching her people. I spontaneously grab her arm. She talks about a woman in her forties who recently came to the Centre and mentioned her parents' and grandparents' racist attitudes. After seeing what went on at the Centre she said, 'From now I'm going to have my own views and break the cycle.'

I'm wrung out by what Narelle and others are dealing with and awed by the commitment of these women. I look around the productive, happy space, paintings on the walls, medical students at work on their canvas, Narelle's grandchildren painting masks, and wonder how it has survived with so little help from outside. Narelle says they also work with police cadets and welfare workers, inviting them to the Centre, explaining their culture through art – attempting to forge a new understanding. They make video clips of elders interacting with school children and I ask Sue if I can come back and observe these. I am sorry not to talk to Lorraine, however, by going with what turned up on the day, I have my own sideways learning experience. I'm mad with myself for not buying Toeweakia's tortoise painting.

***

'Toeweakia's painting's going to Israel!' Narelle calls out as she dances around the art-filled space, though Toeweakia is shy about the attention.

I've come back to talk to Lorraine, but first I need to buy a painting for my grandchildren. I'm pleased to see the one I liked last time is still on the wall: three blue tortoises with green, purple and yellow markings. And I'm happy to be back with my Coomaditchie friends. My first visit to the Centre earlier in the year was unsettling, emotionally draining yet uplifting. Now I've fallen for these women with their loving hearts and strong sense of purpose.

Everything they've gained has been hard-won. The Centre lives from grant to grant with no permanent funding from any section of government. Lorraine, Narelle and Sue, their part-time manager, share one wage. Sue, who is not Aboriginal, acts as a bridge with the wider community, taking care of administrative matters, grant applications and a range of writing requests for everyone who uses the centre. Lorraine uses the word 'bridge' frequently. She sees herself and Narelle as the go-to people. People come to them and they do their best, whatever the request. They've helped provide school tracksuits for sporting trips, made the Centre's phone available for urgent calls, edited job applications and dealt with a range of day-to-day issues arising in their community.

There are large tables covered in art materials, computers for community use, finished paintings tacked onto walls and larger ones resting together on floors. The place has an industrious, happy vibe. I tell Lorraine I like the energy and she says community activities have gone on here for decades. Her husband Sonny Brown remembers them growing up: funerals, weddings, the lot. As I sit talking to Lorraine a stream of young people comes to use computers. Barnardos, the charity that focuses on child protection, donated them and they're in constant demand. Students use them during homework sessions two days per week, reinforcing essential technological skills. People apply for jobs, practise the written component of the driver's licence test and keep in touch with family and friends through social media. The staff are constantly devising new initiatives, often ignoring their own needs. One of the most pressing is that Lorraine needs a walking frame to help her move about.

Community members now work off their fines and do work for the dole here, which pleases Lorraine and Narelle because there are so many projects they need help with. One of them is maintaining the lagoon bush trail, which they built almost single-handedly in 1993, getting rid of mounds of bitou bush and lantana and planting thousands of trees. They run an arts cooperative and raise money for the Centre through the sale of their works. They buy paints when grants come through and believe it's essential to pass on culture to children through art.

They also seek wider engagement with the community. The canvas by the medical students I'd seen earlier in the year, painted under instruction from Narelle, is now finished and waiting for transport to its university home. If people show interest in their culture and ask them to visit, they are ready and happy to be involved. They take part in Naidoc week and are working with the University of Wollongong on a sharing stories project. Lorraine and Narelle recently visited Chesalon Nursing Home at Woonona, where they introduced Indigenous art techniques to the residents and helped them paint a large canvas. The elderly artists were barely able to hold the brushes but loved the experience. The canvas was finished by Lorraine and Narelle and later will be sent on to Chesalon.

They visit schools, tell stories and paint with the children. I ask about relationships with the nearby Kemblawarra Public School and Lorraine tells me about Mr Peters who turned things around in the 1990s. He took the time to come across and ask how the school could work with the community. However, Lorraine worries she is still fighting the same old battles today, trying to get children to go to class. She doesn't know why and wonders if it's a copy-cat problem. School is not easy; Aboriginal students have to deal with racism as they always have. Sonny Brown, Lorraine's husband, hated Port Kembla Public because of the way he was treated. His father came to Port Kembla looking for work after the Second World War and the family lived in sugar bag houses in the sand hills behind

Coomaditchie Lagoon. (I remember seeing this community when I took the shortcut beside the lagoon to the beach during my childhood summers.) Sonny was happier and felt less lonely at the high school because of the greater cultural mix. He was befriended by Italian boys and played soccer with them. The boys' parents also put time and effort into him, which made all the difference and he was grateful for that. His children felt the same about the high school. Lorraine says they learnt Yugoslav and felt at home there. Now the high school is a Senior College, catering for years 10 to 12 only. Years 7 to 9 go to Warrawong High and many from the community are not happy there.

Grants have enabled the women to start new initiatives. Recently they bought computer tablets and children are in the process of recording interviews with their grandparents. Lorraine believes this will encourage younger people to respect and understand their elders. They are hoping to turn the interviews into a documentary to be called 'Connecting Culture'. They are also putting together an arts calendar with a grant from BlueScope Steel.

Before Jenny Briscoe-Hough and Sheryl Wiffin began work at Port Kembla's community centre, Indigenous people felt alienated from the town. They were blamed for everything, mostly by people who had never met them. According to Lorraine, Jenny and Sheryl have broken the ice and Jenny comes to all their meetings. Sheryl's loans initiative for poorer people, the Nils loans, has made a difference, providing money for refrigerators, mowers and other goods. Now the Coomaditchie Centre takes part in festivals and feels less ostracised. Lorraine worries about the continued funding crises. If the Centre closes, the community will only have Centrelink, which they find impersonal and not attuned to their specific needs. She believes the Centre needs guaranteed funding for three workers to keep it running for everybody, but most importantly for the children.

I make plans for my next visit and promise to bring a copy of the book *Streets of Papunya* written by Vivien Johnson and published by my daughter Elspeth. Lorraine says it will help the centre's artists.

# 25
# Looking forward

The town is not done with yet – that's something I've learnt from my visits and meetings with residents. It has the leaders it needs, a spectacular environment and the momentum required to reshape itself into something new and interesting. Residents are reviving old traditions, enlivening the place and attracting visitors back to town. Port people have always invented their own fun, from flying pigeons to wheelbarrow races.

By resuming the annual billy cart race (the first official race was held in 1941), today's residents are tapping into this mood. The *Illawarra Mercury* reports the organiser, Dulcie Dal Molin (who had shown me the old photographs of the town after I met her in the Red Point Cafe) saying, 'Since the first revived race in 2012, Wentworth Street now has boutique wedding shops and an arts precinct.'

My cousin Gordon remembers the 1940s races down Wentworth Street with home-made wooden carts cobbled together with no brakes and wobbly wheels. He said, 'All the kids built one, no doubt with the help of their old man, and the best and faster were those with ball-bearing wheels.'

Peter Darling reckons, 'The best billy cart belonged to Robbie Whitehall whose father owned the bike shop in Wentworth Street. It was made out of old bicycle parts and had a proper steering wheel.'

It wasn't just Port Kembla that was in love with rackety speed. In the mid-twentieth century devotees lugged their carts all over New South Wales in search of a fix. Races were scheduled as part of money raising events for the Patriotic Fund or benefits for local improvements. Derbies were held in Goulburn (the Soap Box Derby, 1952), Mangerton (1953) and Corrimal (1948). The *Illawarra Mercury* described the range of entertainment at Corrimal: wheelbarrow races, musical and vocal items, dancing, pipe and brass bands. The *Southern Mail* (Bowral) noted on 14 September 1951 that billy cart fever was reaching a pitch at the State Final and Commonwealth Jubilee races held at Mount Panorama in Bathurst on the famous circuit.[1] During the 1940s and 50s there were worries about safety. The *Illawarra Mercury* reported children being injured and meetings of councillors discussed safety issues. Action was taken and by the time of the Mangerton Derby, brakes were compulsory.

Zoya Kuptsova and Ryan Phung (2015) *Billy Cart Derby* [screenprint]. Editioned by Thomas Goulder at Duck Print Fine Art Limited Editions for the 2015 Port Kembla Billy Cart Derby.

Today's Port Kembla Derby is a grand affair, attracting many participants and onlookers. It has become an Illawarra tourist attraction. Although the soapbox division is still included, there are exciting new additions: sections for adults, super carts, decorated versions and a grand finale – the street luge, during which organisers hold their collective breath. I visited the November 2015 event. The focused, feverish preparations of the participants created excitement, making up for the small crowd that day. The length of Wentworth Street was lined with plastic barricades to protect racers and spectators and several carts had trouble keeping on track. Paramedics were on hand to apply bandaids to wounded participants. The support teams of fathers and older siblings gathered round the mobile launch pad halfway up the street.

'Ready, set, go!' The man with the microphone called, doing his best to work up the crowd. 'A big round of applause, lots of screaming and yelling, give them some encouragement.' Carts called Bad Influence and Stealth and others attempted to shock and awe the opposition. A billy cart in the shape of a large cake from Tonitto Cakes and a coffin on wheels entered by a local funeral parlour waited their turn in the novelty section. At the top of the street, away from the family fun, were the pros who guarded their sleek, expensive vehicles under tarpaulins. I looked down Wentworth Street past all the fun and saw the not-to-be-forgotten white smoke from the chimney of the Steelworks' coke ovens spiralling into the sky.

The Billy Cart Derby, 2013

## From industrial juggernaut to what?

However, the town will need more than the Billy Cart Derby if it's to prosper. Port Kembla industry is in the doldrums and work is hard to find. The fortunes of the Port Kembla Steelworks are a perfect bell curve. In the 1980s profits rose in a crescendo of production, employing 22,000 workers with three blast furnaces at full capacity. By 2015 there are a mere 3,500 workers maintaining the vast works and only one blast furnace operating. Its trajectory has taken the Steelworks from family-run show to giant multinational, absorbing other businesses on the way, splitting off in 2002 from BHP to become BlueScope. In spite of all this, steelmaking is on the brink, with the real possibility it could fade away altogether. The industrial leviathan may shut up shop – its buildings, chimneys and cranes becoming a huge white elephant, albeit a photogenic one. Decreased demand, cheaper steel coming from China and a deflated yuan have all contributed to Australian steelmaking woes. (One yuan equals 20 cents at time of writing.) It was a different story when steel was king.

In 1938 the *Armidale Express and New England Advertiser* reported that 'Probably at no other part of Australia does the might pulse of industry beat faster than in Port Kembla.'[2] In 2015 this mood has long gone, and uncertainty hovers over Port Kembla and its workers. ER&S/Southern Copper closed in 2003. Now the price of Port Kembla's steel is uncompetitive.

Jobs at BlueScope are threatened and it's understandable why people like George Papaconstantinos are anxious about their future. He survived the massive downturn in the steel industry in 1982, but his father Spiro was not so lucky, and was one of more than 10,000 workers who lost their jobs. Now in his thirty-fifth year at the Port Kembla Steelworks, Mr Papaconstantinos fears what is ahead for BlueScope, where he works as a senior plant operator at the No. 2 blower station, running steam turbines, boilers and blowers. He says, 'We are the heart of the Steelworks. Without the blower station, everything stops ... there would be thousands of people out of work and the effect would be huge.'

In August 2015 the *Sydney Morning Herald* reported a deal offered to workers which BlueScope management called a 'game-changing approach'.[3] The chief executive, Paul O'Malley, gave workers eight weeks to back plans for delivering

$200 million in cost savings, which included 500 job cuts dubbed 'Option A'. He upped the rhetoric by declaring the only alternative was 'Option B', which would mean a complete shutdown of the No. 5 blast furnace, importing raw steel, and the loss of 5,000 direct and indirect jobs. The secretary of the South Coast Labour Council, Arthur Norris, retorted, 'That is not a plan ... it's a threat.'[4]

The whole business of making steel on the South Coast was delicately poised. Early in October 2015 BlueScope steelworkers met and accepted pay cuts and the loss of 500 jobs in order to save the plant. The workers urged the New South Wales premier, Mike Baird, to use local steel for infrastructure projects. The rhetoric coming from government was yes, the steel industry was important, but so too was free trade and being globally competitive.

I wondered what Ted Roach would have done, hero of the 1938 *Dalfram* confrontation. Recently I watched the film *The Dalfram Dispute*, made by Why Documentaries, and was reminded how hard-won reasonable working conditions have been for South Coast workers. Ted broke the bull system that had been used to employ men for work on Port Kembla's wharves. It was a system where only the strongest or sneakiest were chosen and then overworked until they were broken wrecks, exhausted physically and unable to continue working, with no pension or super. The bull system relied on chaos, the men lining up each day and assessed like cattle. Under Roach, a supposedly anarchic communist, all men were given a chance of work, not just the large physical types. The wharves were organised using his disciplined quota system. Port Kembla had never seen the likes of it before. Suzanne Roach, his daughter, said what inspired him was the idea that steps could be taken so everyone could take their own steps.

## New energies

Can the town recapture its buzzy 1950s boom-time feel? There is much to be happy about: a secondary school, a new primary school, a refurbished swimming pool, pollution action groups, an Indigenous centre and a caring, innovative community centre. It's habitable again and different people are coming to live here. I love the story Jenny Briscoe-Hough told me about the primary school, which has a perfect vantage point for spotting whales, and how each classroom has a view of the Tasman Sea. When whales are spotted, a teacher rings the school bell and everyone rushes to watch the breaching whales. I won't draw a comparison with my school experience!

In 2015 Port Kembla Public School is celebrating its 125th anniversary, and the current building is the opposite of the dour, two-storey liver-brick school I attended. It's sleek, the classrooms arranged invitingly around a courtyard. The first person I meet is a retired teacher who likes the place so much she often comes to help. She takes me to reception where I meet Tania and Robyn. Their love of the place is infectious. They confirm the story about the whales – it's Tania who presses the bell. With so many swimming past, nowadays she only presses it when whales are close, and teachers and students assemble on the grass outside her window. The sea is on offer from everywhere I look and clean air floods my lungs as I walk around. I love the library. If you feel like a bit of personal space you can crawl into a wigwam for cosy reading. I notice it's quiet everywhere, unlike most schools. I peep into classrooms which are full of calm, directed group work. Pegged up in one window is a selection of student suggestions on how to approach a dog. There's a tiered permaculture garden full of herbs, vegetables and fruit trees surround the play area. People sometimes take the produce, but as the school has a policy of no fences, wanting people to use the sports facilities at weekends, they accept the occasional theft. Robyn shows me a photo of staff and students on the giant water slide set up in Military Road last summer. The headmaster, Kevin Tucker, is in the middle of it all with a buoy around his waist, ready for action. It's hard to imagine my old headmistress Miss Wade doing anything like that. I like the story about New South Wales Governor David Hurley and his wife joining in the tunnel ball games on their visit to the school as part of the 125-year celebrations. As I leave I take in the low eco-lodge-style building and enveloping seascape and wish I were five and starting over.

***

Evan Salmon has set up his studio in one of the old shops in Wentworth Street, its former life now whitewashed away. There's a sense of ordered creative work: walls are covered in paintings and a quadriptych is arranged on the floor. A large stretcher leans against a shelf waiting for canvas. Charcoal drawings are grouped together pattern-like on one wall and Evan's submission for the 2015 Paddington Art Prize arrests attention near the front door. I'm foisting myself on him, a busy artist with barely enough time to paint as it is, but he's welcoming and allows me to question him about his art and what it is that Port Kembla does to help him create these paintings full of vibrant, colourful energy.

Evan talks about the way he arrived at landscape painting. On a painting trip to Bundanon, the artists' retreat near Nowra, he found traditional landscape painting formless, but he realises now it's something other than bush and rock that inspires him.

'I was always interested in man-made structures and loved the working port around Balmain, where I grew up. This town reminds me of Balmain before it was gentrified.'

He sees connections with still life painting, such as the work of Italian painter and printmaker Giorgio Morandi, and notes that Mondrian painted windmills before moving to abstraction. He suggests the Port's cranes are his equivalent. What he likes about the place is that the structures of crane and wharf were built for purely practical reasons and not designed to be aesthetically pleasing.

'I love the colour of cranes and the escarpment in the distance.'

I look again at his Paddington Art Prize submission and see the arrangement of four separate canvases together juxtaposes structure upon structure, emphasising the variety of shapes. It's energetic, industrial, painted in vibrant colours with touches of brilliant white. The distant green escarpment behind Wollongong is brought closer and helps frame yet form a contrast with the man-made objects. The painting elates me and I'm amazed how strangely new and beautiful the industrial landscape of Port Kembla is when I view it through Evan's eyes.

I have just finished reading Will Self's essay 'Australia and I, A Vexed Relationship'.[5] I looked up a German word he uses to describe his relationship with Australia and it comes close to summing up how I'm feeling about Port Kembla. The word is *unheimlich,* meaning weird or uncanny. What interests me most is the Oxford Dictionary's additional information concerning Freud. It reports that Freud believed what we find weird or uncanny originates not from the exotic or foreign but from what was originally familiar then repressed and subsequently re-manifested in an uncanny *unheimlich* guise. Maybe Evan Salmon's paintings are re-manifesting Port Kembla for me.

Evan Salmon is a slight, shy man and described the night he was announced as winner of the 2015 New South Wales Government's En Plein Air Prize at Parliament House Sydney: 'Suddenly you're up on the podium and expected to be really articulate about what you're doing when you spend most of the time on your own.'

Not that winning prizes ensures a financially secure life. Evan believes there's more support for performing arts than visual arts in the area. He is married to an academic and rents a house in Keira Street that has a panoramic view of the Steelworks and port. He teaches in several of the local TAFEs and is interested when mature age students say they don't know how to draw. He notes we all happily draw as children and have to learn to really look again and be willing to work hard. He says talent sometimes gets in the way, making you headstrong and stubborn. He believes locals have a love-hate relationship with the Steelworks and wonders about its future and that of the town. New people are moving in, real estate prices are going up and one publican owns all the hotels. He wants me to meet the respected printer Tom Goulder, who he says is the reason he is now living in Port Kembla. We knock on the door of Duckprint Fine Art Editions and a head pops out from a window upstairs; it's Tom's son, James.

I love the workshop, with its huge printing presses lined up parallel to each other. On one, a carved wooden plate, about one metre in size, catches my attention. It's the work of Bede Tungutalum, an originator of Tiwi Design. On the wall above is a limited edition ochre and yellow print from this block that has been bought by the Museum of Contemporary Art in Sydney. Another print has been sent to Cambridge University for their art collection. The process seems magical: a painted plate making contact with paper as it passes through the roller press and hey presto! Although occupied, Tom is friendly and ready to explain his processes. He moved his business from Parramatta Road, Camperdown. He studied at the College of Fine Arts (COFA), graduating in 1986. It's a busy place today: an artist is discussing the printing of his work and the walls and shelves are covered with finished prints. We see Evan's 2014 Billy Cart Derby poster. With wheels off the ground and bright colours of red and yellow, it's eye-catching and energetic. I'm intrigued by the old 1890 album printer resting near the door, capable of a run if needed. It's a connection with the old town – it used to belong to Port Kembla Printing. I wonder if I have examples of its work amongst my mother's papers.

Afterwards, walking down Wentworth Street, I see James talking to the graffiti artist, Guido, who has been brought to town to paint the huge wall beside where the Whiteway Theatre once stood. There's a crane partially hiding a half-finished large face. Appropriate, I think: the space may be empty of film, but is still used for creative purposes. The new Port Kembla amazes me: artists and respected printmakers choosing to live here, drawn by the aesthetic attraction of old industry and its relative affordability. Whether these changes are the beginning of a new general prosperity for the town is hard to say, however their presence lifts my spirits.

## Letting the town go

This is hard, so much is unresolved; I want to know what's happening with the funeral project. Are there plans for the ER&S site now copper smelting is finished? Will BlueScope remain in business? Ann Martin's dreams of turning Port Kembla into a tourist hub are beginning to be realised.

In some exciting news, Tender Funerals is close to opening for business. It's moving into the old fire station on Military Road where fire engines once screamed into action, setting off the howling of Peter Darling's dog Brownie. The publicity from the film *Tender* has gained the project wide-ranging support. The Groundswell Project is on board, an organisation that develops arts and health programs that create a cultural change in attitudes to death and dying. Jenny Briscoe-Hough has secured a low-interest loan along with philanthropic funding and there is more than $100,000 donated from the community.

There's hope for the town's main industry, too. 'BlueScope tips $50 million profit boost after job cuts and new Port Kembla enterprise agreement' was a recent headline in the *Sydney Morning Herald*. For now the company's future appears secure. The remaining workers will keep their jobs and the threat of mothballing the No. 5 Blast Furnace has been averted. What's helping is the strong demand for Colorbond and Zincalume products because of the east coast housing boom, and the State government putting on hold the company's $60 million payroll tax bill has relieved some pressure. After the three-year deferral period BlueScope will repay the full amount in increments from 2020 to 2029 on top of normal payroll tax payments. With attention being paid by the Federal government to the dumping of steel by countries like China, which produced 100 tonnes of steel in 2015, and the prioritising of Australian steel in government projects, BlueScope will probably survive.

In 2017 I contacted Craig Nealon, BHP's Communications and Community Manager, and he was reassuring: 'We have no plans for change in the near future. Our next big decision should be in ten years' time when we will need to reline a blast furnace. At the moment we are locked into a fixed production rate (2.6 million tonnes pa) as our blast furnace cannot stop.

Energy prices and inferior imported products are our main challenges.'

I wonder whether any action has occurred as a result of the 60-page *Port Kembla Draft Development Plan* commissioned by the local council and compiled by GHD Pty Ltd in 2007. The plan suggests 'Port Kembla must reinvent itself and the momentum of change needs to be harnessed' without providing specific solutions. Obviously the $140 million being spent on the harbour to accommodate cruise ships will generate work, but the town needs to be reimagined into something exhilarating and prosperous. I'm putting my money on Port Kembla's new batch of enterprising individuals.

I began by writing about ER&S, the copper company which brought my family to Port Kembla. After one hundred years of smelting and refining, all that remains are abandoned buildings and a weed-covered site. Under new management the business changed its name to Port Kembla Copper and was closed in 2003 by its Japanese owners due to weak demand for copper and the rising dollar. Andy Gillespie from the Australian Workers Union (AWU), angry at the loss of 281 jobs, believed ineffective management decisions making during the plant's upgrading in 1997 was the reason the business needed to close.[6]

I'm curious about what will happen to this large piece of old industrial land. It's no surprise investigators found groundwater aquifers were contaminated. But, according to documents tabled at a Wollongong Council meeting on 23 February 2015, that has been fixed. The company wants to move on and has what it calls a 'public positive covenant' for the land. After six years of monitoring, the runoff is judged to be no longer a risk to the ecological receptors living in Port Kembla's outer harbour. There are signs of a changed purpose – the word 'copper' has been dropped from the company's name. It is now called PKC Properties Pty Ltd.

I contacted its CEO, Ian Wilson, in April 2017 and asked about future plans. He told me that part of the site has been leased for car storage and the remaining usable shed stores non-hazardous industrial materials. He presumes the current owners will later sell the property and there will be redevelopment of some kind. I'm hoping that includes an area for community activities such as a park or a place for creative workshops – Ann Martin's dream. The people of Port Kembla have used this site for over a century for work and education and it seems appropriate that a section of the land is set aside for them.

***

I finally catch up with Anne-Louise Rental. It's June 2017 and I'm in the large back room of the Foundry Cafe in Wentworth Street for a women's poetry writing session.

It's Anne-Louise Rental's idea, part of her ongoing project. There are just four of us for the 'I Heard the Mermaids Singing' workshop which has run for a month. I've read about the Indigenous myth of the daughters flung out to sea by their father, becoming the Five Islands. Anne-Louise has developed this idea by imagining them as mermaids. Poet Ali Jane Smith is leading us today and we begin with writing exercises. The aim is to write about the town and I'm surprised what rises to the surface: those who lived parallel lives to mine but had been painted out of memory, and how returning has brought the forgotten bits of the story back into consciousness.

Anne-Louise came to the Illawarra to work at Wollongong's Merrigang Theatre. She received a government grant to develop cultural activities in the area and began by organising a cabaret at the Vault in Port Kembla. Not expecting much of a response, she was amazed on the first night when patrons lined up on the footpath waiting to get in to see the local performers. The cabaret ran from 2003 to 2016. Anne-Louise says that after seeing photos of Wentworth Street in the 1950s, she became obsessed with the street and began gathering its oral history, interviewing as many residents as she could. She is planning a performance in 2018 and has commissioned Ali Jane Smith and Barbara Nicholson to write poetry for the occasion.

26

# A provisional ending

One long Indian summer, that's what my childhood looks like. I wasn't aware of this until I began talking to contemporaries. Everyone loved growing up in Port Kembla in the 1950s and saw their lives as fortunate. Our fathers had jobs, there were houses and gardens in which to play and mothers at home when needed. Lives were simpler – cubs, scouts, tennis, ballet or piano, that was it – the rest of the time was ours. Each night we returned home, happy, replete, our imaginations uncontaminated by television or the internet. What I'd seen as a negative – the lack of cultural amenities – encouraged us to be resourceful.

There was often an anarchic element in our play. A friend Ann was home one summer on holidays from her Sydney boarding school. Her friends wanted a party and chose the Port Kembla Commonwealth Bank as the venue because a father of one of the group was the bank manager and the marble floor and heavy soundproof walls made it perfect for dancing and loud music. The detail that stayed in Ann's mind was not the dancing or flirting or the frisson of being in a bank after hours but a cat walking downstairs from the residence above and dipping its long tail in the inkwells of the desks, turning its fur blue.

I and my contemporaries hurried to leave our birth places, hungry for adventure – the city first and overseas if possible. Saving up, we crammed into windowless cabins and after weeks of sea travel arrived to criss-cross Europe, ticking off galleries, gazing at ruins, giving ourselves the education we thought we lacked. Over time, something happened; the childhood world crept back into our heads and seemed more real than anything else.

Writing about the past is frustrating. I sit waiting, conjuring, hoping, but all that comes are piecemeal, random, vague and at times plain odd memories. There's no detailed, continuous recall. When historians write they have a rich trail to follow: oral, paper and internet. My task has been harder, I don't come from a family of writers. All I had to work with were my mother's 25 pages of handwritten recollections in a small notebook. Other family members wrote nothing down. My only sources have been my imagination, photos, reactivated memories from contemporaries and old local newspapers. Reading the latter has given me the atmosphere and details of the time. The English poet Ted Hughes has likened writing a poem to capturing an animal. It's a visceral experience for him, and the analogy suits me because of my affinity with animals. I've tried following his advice, sniffing out memories, capturing my family and their world and bringing them to life. Because my grandparents lived away from the spotlight and there's no one alive who knew them to confirm the facts, my efforts are just an approximation. My maternal grandparents were quiet, under-the-radar people, unlike my paternal great-grandfather the MP.

The boom and bust history of Port Kembla intrigues me as I was there for the boom part. I'm interested in patterns. The catalyst, coal, was under the ground all along. Mining was good to the town, as was the heavy industry which came in its wake, pollutants aside. The ensuing prosperity made other towns jealous but also impressed. Everyone knew steelmaking was needed for the building boom of the twentieth century. Yet just as suddenly it was all over – market forces and environmental concerns brought it tumbling down. Workers were put off, people left, chimneys were dismantled and ever since the town has been looking for a future.

After recovering from the shock of losing just about every landmark of childhood significance, I like what I've found in Port Kembla during this rediscovery process. It's no longer the wealthy and vibrant industrial town of my childhood but something else – on the cusp of a new future, and the air is fresher! I'm inspired by the people, mostly women, who believe in the place. A town I couldn't get away from quickly enough is drawing me back. I like the combination of remnants of old industry and wide expanses of sea with clouds speeding by in perpetual motion. It's energetic, oppositional. I understand why Frank Hurley found it aesthetically interesting in the 1950s. He's done historians a service with his photos of Wentworth Street that frame for all time the way it was. He saw beauty in the industrial structures surrounding the town, the mounds of coal, chimneys, cranes, the ships in the port. And now artists like Evan Salmon see it too.

I take in the seascape surrounding the town and its Five Islands and remember the myth told by the Alcheringa people. According to them the West Wind lived on the escarpment behind Wollongong with his six daughters. Five of them were always misbehaving. Fed up, he blew them, one at a time, out to sea, and each daughter became an island. The sixth, Geera, fretted and wept, missing her sisters and finally turned into stone. She became Mount Keira.

Many have felt the specialness of the land surrounding Port Kembla. The Buddhists positioned their Berkeley Nan Tien temple to face Mount Kembla and Mount Keira because of the karma there. Aboriginal people have always understood the land's song. My visit to the Coomaditchie Centre makes me hopeful that Aboriginal wisdom will influence how the rest of us view the world. I admire their sideways learning initiative and the way they are fostering a love of the land in their children. To see Coomaditchie Lagoon cleaned up, alive with life, and the tortoise habitat secure makes me hopeful.

The changes from my grandparents' time to mine are unfathomable – from horse and sulky travel to planning permanent homes on Mars. My family's collective memory recalls many firsts. My mother remembers the first car in town and the first radio broadcast; I, the first television. A commentator responding to *Back to the Future*, the 1985 movie which predicted life in 2015, said people imagine a future in fiction and film, creating a desire which activates inventors to finds ways to satisfy it.

I've charted my family's Port Kembla life. Verifying memory is difficult: my cousin Diana loved the local school, I hated it. My recollections are partial, emotional. We each tell a narrative that suits us. Mine has been turned on its head and tested by lack of concrete evidence. My laid-down memories have been shaken. I'm nostalgic for a time I didn't have, one with grandparents living close, yarning to me about their lives, with Gertrude baking cakes and Alfred telling funny stories. I feel closer through writing about them. Return visits to Port Kembla have energised me. I am optimistic about the future. Port Kembla is a punching bag, enough's happened to knock it senseless but, like a down-and-out character who digs deep, it's showing its resilience. Abandoned in the 1950s, reduced to a dormant, yesterday's town, it's fighting back, bolshie and full of life.

I want to see what happens next.

# Epilogue: Aunty Barbara

There's one more person I need to talk to before I finish – Barbara Nicholson. She's an elder of the Wadi-Wadi people – Port Kembla was built on their land. For decades she's taught her people's law and culture at several universities and for 11 years has been a member of Wollongong University's ethics committee. She is passionately involved in a range of issues concerning her people: deaths in custody, incarceration rates among Aboriginal people, land rights, and she teaches writing to gaol inmates. Wollongong University awarded her an honorary Doctorate of Law in recognition of her work in 2014. She's a phenomenon and I want to meet her.

'I was living in a village west of Lake Macquarie dominated by the Seventh Day Adventist Church. It took them five years to say hello,' Barbara tells me. 'I made a friend, Diane – we were always yarning. One day I said to her, I'm going to have to do something, go to work, go mad or go to school.'

We're in Barbara's snug and tidy house in Port Kembla, talking, drinking tea and eating Anzac biscuits the day after Anzac Day. Kelly, a helper from Aboriginal Services, is also there. 'I came to look after Barbara and she looks after me.' Phones are ringing, plans are being made – Barbara is off shortly on a writing retreat. Barbara is telling me how she started university.

'A friend rang one day, "Do you want to come for a run to Newcastle?" Outside the university, which is on the way, she said, "I have to duck in here for a while, why don't you come?"

'"Too hot," I said, but she talked me into it. We went down to the basement of the Faculty of Arts where there was a sign saying, "Community Programs". She bashed on the door and called out as she opened it, "Here she is." She'd set it up. It was Friday and the mature age entry course started on Monday.'

Barbara shows me copies of four volumes of *Dreaming Inside*, the results of her creative writing course at Junee Correctional Centre. "I can't write, Aunty," they said. It was like extracting molars.' There were only four contributors in the first volume. The fifth volume, being launched on 25 May 2017 at Wollongong Art Gallery, has 60. 'It's my initiative, my baby and I drive it.'

I turn the conversation to Port Kembla's history and say, 'My mother remembers the first car in town – it belonged to the Pratts.'

'No, that's not right, it belonged to my mother. She was the first female to get a driving licence in New South Wales. My mother had resources.'

I let that one go, memory's tricky and as Barbara says, a mixed bag. Her sister and I were born at the same maternity hospital in Donaldson Street and the same nurse, Nurse Lovelock, helped us into the world. I went home to Robertson

Street and she to the reserve – living there with her mother, a non-Indigenous woman, and her stepfather. The Kemblawarra reserve covered land from Shellharbour Road, including Coomaditchie Lagoon, and finished at Port Kembla Beach. Barbara's people, the Wadi-Wadi, also lived for thousands of years on the land to the east, known as Hill 60, but were removed during the Second World War by the Army who appropriated it to build barracks and gunnery positions. They were never allowed to return.

There wasn't much to like about Port Kembla Catholic school, according to Barbara (this was the school I used to envy my friend Sue going to). Barbara was expelled at the age of four. The teachers wouldn't let her go to the toilet so she urinated into a cup. She returned when she was a little older. Lessons were held in the church, the older students facing the altar and the younger ones facing the back. The children from the camp arrived bare-footed, their feet covered in black sand. Before they were allowed into class they were taken to a tap outside the convent where 'a nun stripped us down to our knickers and washed us to make us hygienic'. Not until Sixth Class did Barbara have a teacher she liked. Her name was Sister Honorina.

'In the forties we were dirt poor, there was no sanitation, garbage collection, electricity or water on the reserve.' Her mother didn't receive a widow's pension until months after the death of Barbara's stepfather and Barbara received an exemption from high school to begin work at Fairleys in Port Kembla. 'Bobby Pins to Battleships' was their slogan, she remembers. I was five when Barbara was 13. She was probably working there when my mother and I did our shopping.

'There was never any money and if we wanted to go to the pictures, we had two ways of getting some. One was to pick gum tips and hawk it for 1-penny and 3-penny bunches in Bland and Robertson Streets, where posh people lived. If we got 6 to 9 pence we were happy – we could go to the pictures and have some over to buy a 1 penny ice-cream. The other way was to collect beer bottles. We scouted around – if we couldn't find any we went out the back of Lindsay's Pub (Top Pub), found some and cashed them in. Charlie Anderson was the theatre manager at the Whiteway and told us we could only sit in peanut alley. You paid extra for up in the gods. Sometimes the boys collected yellow cake from Fertilisers and made stink bombs, letting them off in the theatre.

'We lived mainly on the beach or at the lake. There was sustenance there – we dived, got prawns and mutton fish. We jagged mullet. They are bottom swimmers, coming to the top in autumn. You get mullet best with big hooks – at least three together at the end of the line. You toss it into the water with sinkers and jag the line back when you've hooked the fish. At the lake we'd fill a kerosene tin with prawns, light a fire underneath, fill the tin with clean salt water, cook them and eat the whole bloody lot. Then we'd get another tin-full and take them home for breakfast. Now there are more people fishing than prawns. It's scandalous what they're doing at the entrance, a lake needs to silt up. There'll be a five-star Hotel Utopia out on the island soon.'

We talk for two hours. I want to bring up Queen Rosie's name. She worked for my grandmother and was remembered fondly by my mother, but I'm hesitant because she was their queen, yet employed by my family to do their washing. I say her name.

'She was my great-grandmother.'

We relax, the overlaps amaze us. Barbara asks for more details and I tell her what I know. She says Micky, Rosie's husband, wasn't Wadi-Wadi. He had been kidnapped and forced into service as a small boy on a ship. After he was dumped off La Perouse he made his way to Port Kembla. Barbara says she's happy I'm including her people in my account. I say what worries me is how to do it without offending. She tells me about the protocols for naming Aboriginal people. Barbara explains that in her culture names belong to the whole family and I will need to ask for permission before I use them.

'What about the socio-political?' Two hours into our conversation, with my husband waiting outside in the car with only the newspaper for company and we are getting to the heart of the matter. Barbara and supporters lodged a native title claim over 32 acres, including Coomaditchie Lagoon, but were unsuccessful. According to the court, because the land had been given as a grant in 1812 to a farmer, this extinguished any native title claim. Barbara hasn't given up. She says as it's now crown land this should override the land grant argument and the claim needs to be reconsidered.

I drag myself away, we return for more hugs. I'm emotional – it's one of the most moving meetings of my life. Barbara comes out to give my husband a wave. I feel Humpy Dumpty-like – put back together with all the bits in the right place. I see now how my family's life ran parallel to Barbara's.

As Barbara says. 'You can't change the past but you sure can do something about the future.'

# Acknowledgments and sources

I'm indebted to Trove and in particular back copies of the *Illawarra Mercury*. They gave me names, descriptions of standout events as well as fascinating side stories. It's where I sensed the mood of the times, how people were affected and what mattered most to them. I learnt details of life that helped verify family stories. The paper began publishing in the Illawarra in 1885 and is the second-oldest regional newspaper in New South Wales. In 1968 it merged with the *South Coast Times*, another of my essential sources. I'm grateful a reporter from the *South Coast Times* was present at the opening of the Port Kembla baths in 1937. Because of him I know about larger-than-life Mr Spooner and the lives of the people of the Port and their resourcefulness.

To all the people I have talked to about Port Kembla, thank you for your insights and good humour, including my brother, David Nock; cousins Diana Armstrong and Gordon Hartley; and Anne Mitchell, Peter Darling, Jenny Briscoe-Hough, Cheryl Wiffin, Gerard Willems, Michael Fix, Sheila Hoskins, Brian Jackson, Barbara Gassman, Ann Martin, Helen Hamilton, Nella Keenan, Evan Salmon, Tom Goulder, Glen Mitchell, Lorraine Brown and her sister Narelle, and

Barbara Nicholson. Thank you to Ron Pretty and Rike Krishnabhakdi-Vasilakis at the South Coast Writers Centre for suggestions, and to Linda Funnell for her forensic editing skills. Thanks to the staff of Wollongong Library who were always happy to deal with my barrage of queries, to my friend, Nicholas Pounder, for his publishing guidance, and to Nick Walker, Anastasia Buryak and Wayne Saunders at Australian Scholarly Publishing.

Thank you to Michael Fix for permission to quote from the song 'Copper Town Blues' (Michael Fix, Mark Cryle – Control) on his album *Lines and Spaces*.

Thank you to Zoya Kuptsova and Ryan Phung for permission to use their 2015 Port Kembla Billy Cart Derby poster.

The extract from 'Aboriginal Women's Heritage' is reproduced with permission from Louise Davis and the NSW Office of Environment and Heritage.

A special thank you to my husband John and daughter Elspeth for your patience and willingness to listen at every stage of the process.

# Bibliography

Banks, B. (ed.), *Port Kembla Public School Centenary 1890–1990.*

Dykes, O., *Port Kembla 1770–1992*, Port Kembla Mission Committee, 1992.

Eklund, E.C., *Steel Town: The Making and Breaking of Port Kembla*, Melbourne University Press, 2002.

GHD Pty Ltd, *Draft Port Kembla Main Street, Future Vision and Desired Character Report*, October 2007.

McDonald, W.G. (ed.), *Earliest Illawarra By Its Explorers and Pioneers*, Illawarra Historical Society, 1966.

McPhillips, K. (ed.), *Local Heroes*, Pluto Press, Annandale New South Wales, 2002.

Mitchell, G., *'Work and Community: The Port Kembla copper smelter, 1900–1920. Illawarra Unity', Journal of the Illawarra Branch of the Australian Society for the Study of Labour History*, Vol. 2, No. 1, 1999.

Mitchell, G., 'Vincent Wardell 1903–1990', *Australian Dictionary of Biography*, Vol. 18, Melbourne University Press, 2012.

Reynolds, D.K., *A History of the Land Purchased for the Building of the Port Kembla Steelworks*, BHP Flat Products, 2001.

# Notes

## 2 – Going back in 2015

1 Lynette Wallworth, *Tender*, Scarlett Pictures 2013.

2 Glen Humphries, 'Port Kembla school destroyed by inferno', *Illawarra Mercury*, 4 January 2013.

3 George Blaxell, 'Port Kembla Harbour', *Discovery to the Inner Harbour Part 2*.

## 3 – 1910: My family comes to town

1 *Illawarra Mercury*, 4 March 1921.

2 See http://www.bealepianos.com.au.

3 *Illawarra Mercury*, 11 March 1913.

## 4 – Other people in the landscape

1 Extract from Lt James Cook's journal (1770) from *Earliest Illawarra* 1966.

2 Extract from Matthew Flinders' journal (1796) from *Earliest Illawarra* 1966.

3 Letter from John Campbell to John Oxley, 16 November 1816 from *Earliest Illawarra* 1966, p. 31.

4 Aboriginal Women's Heritage Department of Environment and Conservation New South Wales Report, 2014.

## 5 – Boom times round the corner

1 Samuel Beckett *Waiting for Godot*, Act 2.

2 *Illawarra Mercury*, 30 May 1896.

3 *Sydney Morning Herald*, 22 July 1902.

4 *Illawarra Mercury*, 8 August 1896.

## 6 – Nothing's stopping them

1 *South Coast Times and Wollongong Argus*, 24 February 1911.

2 'World War I: Snapshot of Australia at the time of the outbreak', ABC online: http://www.abc.net.au/news/2014-08-04/world-war-i-snapshot-australia-time-of-outbreak/5634632.

3 *South Coast Times*, 4 July 1917.

4 *South Coast Times*, September 1951.

## 7 – Life for the more fortunate 1910–1930

1 *South Coast Times*, 21 May 1921.

## 8 – First World War and aftermath

1 *Illawarra Mercury*, 22 December 1916.

## 10 – Boom times

1 DK Reynolds, *A History of the Land Purchased for the Building of the Port Kembla Steelworks*, 2001.

2 *Sydney Morning Herald*, 21 April 1919.

3 *North West Champion*, 18 March 1937.

## 11 – 1930s: Depression and beyond

1 *Sydney Morning Herald*, 22 January 1938.

2 *Sydney Morning Herald*, 1 November 1944.

3 *Illawarra Mercury*, 28 August 1931.

4 *Illawarra Mercury*, 17 July 1931.

5 *South Coast Times*, 26 August 1932.

6 *South Coast Times*, 26 February 1937.

7 *South Coast Times*, 26 February 1937.

## 12 – Audrey and Doug

1 *South Coast Times*, 14 June 1945.

2 *Illawarra Mercury*, March 1939.

## 13 – Steelmaking and my father

1 J. Hagan and A. Wells (eds.), *Changing Economics and the Labour Movement, A History of Wollongong*, 1997.

## 14 – 1940s: Port Kembla and war

1 The Lysaght company began in Bristol in 1857 when John Lysaght opened a small galvanising works. From these beginnings it morphed into a large Australian sheet rolling and galvanising business first based first in Newcastle (1921) and then Port Kembla (1936). The Port Kembla works was later absorbed into BlueScope Steel in 1979 and the name changed in 2003 to BlueScope Lysaght.

2 Glenn Mitchell 'Wardell, Vincent (Aloysius) Andrew (1903–1990)' *Australian Dictionary of Biography* Vol. 18, MUP, 2012.

3 P Darling, *Portrait of a Nurse*, Don Wall, 2001.

4 Obituary, *Sydney Morning Herald*, 12 December 2007.

5 'Port Kembla RSL Goes Up for Sale', *Illawarra Mercury*, 16 January 2017.

## 15 – Movers and shakers

1 *Sunday Times*, 5 January 1930.

## 16 – A 1950s snapshot

1 The amalgamation of the councils in 1947 was seen as a step forward by much of the region, but Port Kembla residents believed their concerns were less likely to be heard in this

much larger body. See EC Eklund, *Steel Town: The Making and Breaking of Port Kembla*, 2002.

2 My father admired Essengton Lewis, they both came from South Australia but, it was Lewis's commitment to steelmaking and all things metal that really impressed him. At the time Lewis was Australia's leading industrialist. He was appointed General Manager of BHP in 1921 and spent his life investigating the process of making steel. His abilities were recognised by Robert Menzies when he appointed him Director of Munitions during the Second World War.

3 *Sydney Morning Herald*, 17 October 1950.

## 18 – Beaches of the Port

1 *Metal Manufactures Gazette*, 1964.

2 *Sydney Morning Herald*, 10 February 1963.

## 19 – 1950s and the outside world

1 *Illawarra Mercury*, 13 February 2011.

2 *Illawarra Mercury*, 22 March 2015.

## 20 – 1950s Stand-out events

1 Wollongong Theatre Pty Ltd, 1954, National Film and Sound Archive.

## 21 – Exodus

1 *Illawarra Mercury*, 13 May 1948.

2 *Illawarra Mercury*, 19 February 2014.

3 *Illawarra Mercury*, 18 February 1959.

4 *Illawarra Mercury*, March 1965.

5 *Cancer and Industrial Pollution*, an ongoing investigation by the Socialist Equality Party 1997, http://www.sep.org.au/cancer/index.htm.

## 22 – 2014: Demolition day

1 Gemma Khaicy, 'Getting Ready for Port Kembla Stack Demolition', *Illawarra Mercury*, 13 February 2014.

2 Ibid.

3 Lucy Marks, 'Port Kembla Grandmothers Helen Hamilton and Olive Rodwell join forces in lifelong fight for change', ABC, 12 August 2015.

4 Andre Carswell and Leigh Van Den Brocke, 'Vibrations worry residents after explosives bring Port Kembla stack down', *Daily Telegraph*, 20 February 2014.

5 Michael Fix, 'Coppertown Blues', from his album *Lines and Spaces*, 2014.

## 23 – Women of the Port

1 'How these women cleaned up the Port', *Illawarra Mercury*, February 2014.

2 'Passage of Change', *Open Road*, March–April 2017.

## 24 – Coomaditchie women

1 *Coomaditchie* by Lorraine Brown, a digital story from the Lake Illawarra MAP Project. https://www.youtube.com/watch?v=ELddS1Jc3fo.

## 25 – Looking forward

1 *Southern Mail* (Bowral),14 September 1951.

2 *Armidale Express and New England Advertiser*, 5 September 1938.

3 *Sydney Morning Herald*, 13 August 2015.

4 *Sydney Morning Herald*, 31 August 2015.

5 *The Monthly*, October 2015.

6 *Sydney Morning Herald*, 28 July 2003

www.ingramcontent.com/pod-product-compliance
Ingram Content Group Australia Pty Ltd
76 Discovery Rd, Dandenong South VIC 3175, AU
AUHW021028021225
420336AU00004B/75

9 781925 801590